The Olympics'
Most Wanted

Also by Floyd Conner

Baseball's Most Wanted
More Baseball's Most Wanted
Football's Most Wanted
Basketball's Most Wanted
Golf's Most Wanted
Hockey's Most Wanted
Tennis's Most Wanted
Wrestling's Most Wanted

The Olympics' Most Wanted

The Top 10 Book of Gold Medal Gaffes, Improbable Triumphs, and Other Oddities

Floyd Conner

Brassey's, Inc.

WASHINGTON, D.C.

Library of Congress Cataloging-in-Publication Data

Conner, Floyd, 1951–
   The Olympics' most wanted : the top 10 book of
gold medal gaffes, improbable triumphs, and
other oddities / Floyd Conner.– 1st ed.
      p.   cm.
   Includes bibliographical references and index.
   ISBN 1-57488-413-1 (alk. paper)
   1. Olympics–Miscellanea. 2. Athletes–Anecdotes.
   I. Title.

GV721.7 .C66 2001
796.48–dc21

                                                  2001043524

Printed in Canada on acid-free
paper that meets the American National Standards
Institute Z39-48 Standard.

Brassey's, Inc.
22841 Quicksilver Drive
Dulles, Virginia 20166

Designed by Pen & Palette Unlimited.

First Edition

10 9 8 7 6 5 4 3 2 1

Contents

List of Photographs

Introduction

The ancient Olympic Games were held in Olympia, Greece, from 776 B.C. to A.D. 393. In 1896, the first modern Olympic Games took place in Athens. Except for interruptions due to World Wars I and II, the Summer Olympics have been contested every four years. The Winter Olympics were created in 1924. The 2002 Winter Olympics will be staged in Salt Lake City.

Olympics' Most Wanted salutes the Games' most outstanding offenders. The book contains top ten lists of the worst athletes, poorest officiating, and biggest blunders in Olympic history. The lists feature the most unlikely heroes, biggest disappointments, craziest fans, strangest competitions, and the weirdest things ever to occur at the Olympics.

Some Olympic performances border on the unbelievable. Margaret Abbott won the women's golf competition at the 1900 Paris Olympics without even realizing she was competing in the Olympics. George Lyon, the men's golf champion at the 1904 Olympics, walked on his hands at the victory ceremony. At the 1928 Olympics, rower Henry Pearce stopped to let a line of ducks swim in front of his boat and still won the race. Cyclists Giovanni Pettenella and Pierre

Trentin stayed motionless for 22 minutes during their 1,000-meter sprint race at the 1964 Olympics.

Over the years there have been some unusual Olympic competitions. At the 1896 Athens Olympics, the 100-meter freestyle swimming competition was limited exclusively to sailors in the Greek navy. The 1900 Paris Olympics featured a live pigeon-shooting competition and a 200-meter obstacle-course swimming event. Four years later in St. Louis, the Games included a mud-fighting competition and an all-around dumbbell contest. The strangest event at the 1906 Athens Games was dueling pistols.

Not every Olympic competitor can be a champion. Antoin Miliordos of Greece fell 18 times during a slalom run at the 1952 Winter Olympics. Perhaps the slowest skier in Olympic history was Turkey's Resat Erces, who averaged a snail-like five miles per hour during a downhill run at the 1936 Winter Olympics. South Korean Kyung Soon-yim had never skied on snow prior to competing in the slalom at the 1960 Squaw Valley Winter Games. He had learned to ski by reading instructional books and practiced on grass. Eric Moussambani, a swimmer from Equatorial Guinea, was so slow in a 100-meter qualifying heat at the 2000 Sydney Olympics that an announcer nearly jumped into the pool because he thought he was drowning.

Bob Hayes, the gold medalist in the men's 100-meter dash at the 1964 Olympics, was known as The World's Fastest Human. Not every Olympic athlete has such a complimentary nickname. American cyclist Nash McCrea was nicknamed Crash because he caused several collisions at the 1904 Olympics. Ray Ewry, a ten-time gold medalist in standing high-jump competitions, was nicknamed The Human Frog. Legendary Czech runner Emil Zátopek was called The

Beast of Prague because he grimaced and rolled his eyes while running. Inept British ski jumper Eddie Edwards was known as Eddie the Eagle, a jab at his less-than-soaring leaps.

The Olympics have had more than their share of colorful characters. Skier Diana Gordon-Lennox wore a monocle and competed with her leg in a cast at the 1936 Winter Olympics. Italian Ugo Frigero, a double gold medalist in walking events at the 1920 Olympics, directed the stadium musicians by waving his arms while competing. Marja Lilsa-Hämäläinen, the winner of three gold medals in cross-country skiing at the 1984 Winter Olympics, was so publicity shy that she ran and hid from reporters after each victory. Glynis Nunn of Australia, the 1984 gold medalist in the women's heptathlon, had to overcome a mental block about crossing the finish line.

Athletes at the ancient Games competed in the nude. At the 1908 London Olympics, American runners were threatened with disqualification if they wore white shorts. Abebe Bikila of Ethiopia won the marathon at the 1960 Rome Olympics while running barefoot. At the 1988 Calgary Winter Olympics, officials forced sexy East German figure skater Katarina Witt to add feathers to one of her revealing outfits. Algeria's Hassiba Boulmerka, the women's 1,500-meter gold medalist at the 1992 Olympics, was criticized in her own country for running bare-legged in front of thousands of men.

Olympic athletes have eaten and drunk some pretty strange things. During the 1904 marathon, Cuban runner Félix Carbajal developed stomach cramps after stopping to pick and eat green apples during the race. In that same race, winner Thomas Hicks was administered a dose of strychnine sulfate in egg whites to enhance his performance. After consuming a large meal prior to competing in the 10,000 meters at the 1920 Olympics, Frenchman Joseph Guillemot vomited on the shoes of his rival, Paavo Nurmi. Runner Gabriella Doria, the women's 1,500-meter gold medalist at the 1984 Olympics, bathed in wine to celebrate her victory.

Some athletes will do anything for a gold medal. In the 1904 St. Louis Olympics, American marathoner Fred Lorz rode 11 of the 26 miles in an automobile. When Stella Walsh, winner of the women's 100-meter dash at the 1932 Los Angeles Olympics, was murdered in 1980, it was discovered that she was really a man. Boris Onischencko, a Soviet pentathlete at the 1976 Montreal Olympics, rigged his épée to falsely register touches.

Athletes have been disqualified for some odd reasons. Gehnäll Persson of Sweden had to return his gold medal from the 1948 equestrian dressage competition because officials learned that he was a non-commissioned officer. Iranian boxer Ali Kazemi was disqualified at the 1992 Barcelona Olympics because he forgot to bring his boxing gloves to the ring. At those same Games, Canadian yachtsman Hank Lammens was disqualified for not remembering to bring his life jacket.

This book introduces you to more than 600 of the Olympics' most wanted athletes. Their offenses range from inept performances to outrageous behavior. Be on the lookout for these individuals.

The Opening Ceremonies

Let's begin by reviewing notable Summer and Winter Olympic firsts.

1. COROEBUS

The inaugural Olympic Games were held in Greece in 776 B.C. The first Olympic champion was a young Greek runner named Coroebus. The only event was a sprint of approximately 170 meters. As his reward, Coroebus was crowned with a wreath made from the leaves of an olive tree that grew near the Temple of Zeus in Olympia. According to legend, the tree had been planted by Hercules.

2. FRANCIS LANE

The first race of the modern Olympics in Athens, Greece, was a qualifying heat for the 100-meter dash. American Francis Lane won the heat in a time of 12.2 seconds. The final of the 100-meter dash was run on April 10, 1896. Lane finished third as another American, Thomas Burke, won in a time of 12.0 seconds.

3. JAMES CONNOLLY

James Connolly of the United States had the distinction of being the first Olympic champion. On April 6, 1896, Connolly finished first in the hop, step, and jump. Connolly's winning jumps measured 44 feet, 11 inches, more than three feet farther than second-place finisher Alexandre Tuffère of France. The event is now known as the triple jump.

4. CHARLOTTE COOPER

The first woman Olympic champion was British tennis player Charlotte Cooper. She defeated Hélène Prévost of France 6–1, 6–4 in the championship match played on July 11, 1900. Cooper, a five-time Wimbledon champion, also won the mixed doubles with partner Reginald Doherty.

5. ELIZABETH ROBINSON

The first Olympic track-and-field competition for women was the 100-meter sprint held on July 31, 1928, in Amsterdam. The winner was Elizabeth Robinson, a 16-year-old from Illinois. Robinson had competed in her first track meet only four months prior to the Olympics. A natural athlete, she set a world record in her second race. Robinson was so nervous prior to the gold-medal heat that she brought two left shoes to the track. She had to run back to retrieve her right shoe.

In 1931, Robinson was nearly killed in a plane crash. The first person to arrive at the scene of the accident was so certain she was dead that he placed her in his trunk and drove her to the local mortician. Amazingly, Robinson survived, but she was in a coma for nearly two months. Her injuries included a concussion, lacerated forehead, broken leg, and fractured hip. Her leg did not heal properly, and it was doubtful she would ever walk again. But Robinson never gave up, and her miraculous recovery culminated in 1936 in Berlin when she won a second gold medal as a member of the American 4×100-meter relay team.

6. EWA KLOBUKOWSKA

Ewa Klobukowska won a bronze medal in the women's 100-meter dash at the 1964 Olympics. Klobukowska also won a gold medal as a member of the Polish 4×100-meter relay team. In 1967, Klobukowska became the first Olympic gold medalist to fail a sex chromosome test. Though she possessed female genitalia and reproductive organs, a rare medical condition caused her to have XXY chromosomes. Her gold medals were stripped as a result.

7. CHRISTA ROTHENBURGER

Christa Rothenburger of the German Democratic Republic was the gold medalist in the 500-meter speed-skating event at the 1984 Winter Olympics. At the 1988 Games in Calgary, Canada, she finished first in the 1,000-meter speed-skating competition. At the 1988 Summer Olympics in Seoul, South Korea, she won the silver medal in the 1,000-meter match sprint cycling race, becoming the first athlete to win a medal in both the Winter and Summer Olympics in the same year.

8. ALEKSANDR DITYATIN

The first athlete to win eight medals at a single Olympics was Soviet gymnast Aleksandr Dityatin. He was a medalist in every gymnastic event at the 1980 Moscow Olympics. Dityatin won three gold, four silver, and one bronze medal.

9. DICK BUTTON

American figure skater Dick Button won the gold medal at the 1948 and 1952 Winter Olympics. At the 1948 Olympics in St. Moritz, Switzerland, Button landed the first double axel, a two-and-a-half-revolution jump. Four years later at the Oslo Winter Games, Button landed the first triple jump in competition, a triple loop. What made the achievement even more impressive was that he attempted the triple-loop jump first instead of the easier triple toe loop or triple salchow.

10. PETR BARNA

Forty years after Dick Button landed the first triple jump, Petr Barna of Czechoslovakia landed the first four-revolution jump in Olympic history. Barna included a quadruple toe loop in his long program at the Games in Albertville, France. Despite the historic jump, Barna finished third behind Victor Petrenko of the United Team (Soviet Union) and American Paul Wylie.

The Ancient Games

The first ancient Olympic Games were staged in 776 B.C. in Olympia, Greece. The Games were created as a religious festival. The first Olympics consisted of only one event, the stade, a sprint race of less than 200 meters. Over the years, other events were added, including tehrippon (a four-horse chariot race), pankration (wrestling), and boxing. Olympic champions were often considered gods and dedicated life-size bronze statues to themselves. Winners were crowned with olive wreaths and presented with palm branches. The hometowns of the champions sometimes honored them by knocking a hole in the protective walls of their cities to allow the champions to drive through the openings in a chariot.

Athletes from as far away as Spain and Africa competed in the Games. All the athletes competed nude, although there was a foot race, the hoplitodromia, for runners in armor. The lampadedromia, a relay race in which the runners carried a torch, inspired the Olympic torch that is used today to light the Olympic flame. The Games were held in such high regard that truces were often instituted to allow athletes from warring nations to compete. The Olympics were held every four years for more than 1,100 years. In A.D. 393, the Christian Roman Emperor Theodosius I prohibited pagan worship and effectively brought an end to the ancient Olympic Games.

1. APOLLONIUS THE SPRINKLER

In A.D. 93, a boxer named Apollonius the Sprinkler arrived late for his match. He claimed that his arrival had been delayed by Aegean winds during his voyage. Apollonius was disqualified when it was learned that he was late because he had been competing in games in Asia. The olive wreath was awarded to his opponent, Heraclides.

2. KYNISKA OF SPARTA

Married women were not permitted to attend the ancient Games. Only virgins were considered pure enough to witness the sacred rites. A married woman faced the penalty of death if she was caught observing the Games. The first female Olympic champion was Kyniska of Sparta. She owned the horses that won the tethrippon in 396 B.C. In those days, the prize was awarded not to the driver of the chariot, but to the owner of the horses.

3. MELANKOMAS OF CARIA

Ancient boxing matches were brutal encounters that could last for hours. Melankomas of Caria was the Muhammed Ali of his time. A champion in the first century A.D., he boasted that he could keep up his guard for two days straight. Melankomas danced around his opponents, rarely throwing a punch, until the frustrated boxers were exhausted from trying to corner the elusive target. The vain boxer boasted that, despite many bouts, his face remained unmarked.

4. CLEOMEDES OF ASTYPALAEA

Cleomedes was a feared boxer from the Aegean island of Astypalaea. In 492 B.C., an opponent died after receiving a brutal beating from Cleomedes. The victorious boxer was disqualified, not for killing his opponent, but for a foul that occurred during the bout. Cleomedes was so distraught at being denied his Olympic title that he went mad.

5. ALYTES AND MASTIGOPHORAI

The penalties for breaking rules at the ancient Games ranged from fines to physical punishment. Athletes charged with less serious infractions were fined. The monies collected were used to finance the statues adorning the Olympic stadium. More serious offenders were flogged by whip bearers, known as the mastigophorai. Runners who were charged with a false start were whipped by officials known as the alytes.

6. MILON OF KROTON

Wrestler Milon of Kroton was a five-time Olympic champion. A man of enormous appetites, he reportedly ate an entire calf prior to one of his matches. His incredible strength contributed to his death. According to legend, he tried to pull apart a tree that had been partially split. His hands became caught in the narrow opening, and, defenseless, Milon was attacked and devoured by wild animals.

7. APENE

The chariot races were one of the highlights of the ancient Games. A less glamorous event was the apene, a 17-mule cart race. The apene was an event in 14 Olympiads, beginning around 500 B.C.

8. SOSTRATOS OF SIKYON

The pankration wrestling event was one of the most dangerous of the Olympic competitions. Punching and choking were permitted, and wrestlers applied arm holds and leg locks that twisted limbs out of their sockets. One wrestler, Polydamas of Skotussa, strangled a lion with his hands. Another grappler, Sarapion of Alexandria, was so terrified of his opponent that he ran away on the day before the match. The brutal Sostratos of Sikyon was universally feared. Nicknamed Mr. Finger Tips, he broke his opponents' fingers to make them submit.

9. LEONIDAS OF RHODES

Perhaps the greatest runner in the ancient Games was Leonidas of Rhodes. He won every race contested at the four Olympiads held between 164 B.C. and 152 B.C. The 12 races he won ranged from sprints of less than 200 meters to middle-distance races of nearly 5,000 meters.

10. SACRIFICES

Because early Olympic Games were considered to be religious festivals, animal sacrifices were common. Up to 100 oxen were slaughtered and burned in honor of Greek gods. Occasionally athletes would consult the internal organs of the slain beasts to see if they foretold victory.

Running for Office

M any Olympic heroes have gone on to political careers. Chi Cheng, the 1968 bronze medalist in the women's 100-meter dash, was elected to the Taiwanese parliament in 1981. The gold medalist in the javelin at the 1972 and 1976 Olympics, Ruth Fuchs, was a member of the East German parliament. Rosa Mota, the 1988 marathon champion, was elected to the Portuguese parliament in 1995.

1. BILL BRADLEY

Bill Bradley was an All-American basketball player at Princeton University. He starred on the gold-medal-winning 1964 United States basketball team. Bradley played for ten seasons in the National Basketball Association with the New York Knicks. He played on NBA championship teams in 1970 and 1973. In 1978, Bradley was elected to the House of Representatives and later served in the United States Senate, representing the state of New Jersey. He made an unsuccessful run for the 2000 Democratic presidential nomination.

2. PHILLIP NOËL-BAKER

Englishman Phillip Noël-Baker won a silver medal in the 1,500-meter run at the 1920 Antwerp Olympics. Baker was a member of the British parliament for 36 years. A devout pacifist, he won the Nobel Peace Prize in 1959 in recognition of his work to further disarmament.

3. BEN NIGHTHORSE CAMPBELL

Ben Nighthorse Campbell was the captain of the 1964 United States Olympic judo team. In 1986, he was elected to the House of Representatives. Six years later, Campbell was elected to the United States Senate representing the state of Colorado.

4. LORD DAVID BURGHLEY

David Burghley of Great Britain won the gold medal in the 1928 400-meter hurdles. Three years later, Burghley was elected to the parliament. He also served as governor of Bermuda.

5. BOB MATHIAS

Seventeen-year-old Bob Mathias won the decathlon at the 1948 London Olympics. Four years later, he repeated as decathlon champion. In 1966, Mathias was elected to Congress representing California's eighteenth district and went on to serve four terms in the House of Representatives.

6. TOM MCMILLEN

Tom McMillen played on the 1972 United States Olympic basketball team that won the silver medal. He played 11 seasons in the NBA. McMillen was elected to Congress representing Maryland in 1986.

7. RALPH METCALFE

Ralph Metcalfe won a silver medal in the 100-meter dash and a bronze medal in the 200-meter dash at the 1932 Los Angeles Olympics. During the 1970s, Metcalfe served in the United States House of Representatives.

8. HIROFUMI DAIMATSU

Hirofumi Daimatsu, coach of the 1964 gold-medal-winning Japanese women's volleyball team, was notorious for his demanding training regimen. Daimatsu insisted that players train six hours a day, seven days a week. He did not permit dating, believing that it might break the athletes' concentration. Daimatsu intimidated his players with verbal and physical abuse. He drove them to tears with insults and was even known to hit and kick them. Four years after his team's Olympic victory, Daimatsu was elected to the House of Councilors in the Japanese parliament.

9. JOHN PIUS BOLAND

In 1896, Irishman John Pius Boland traveled to Athens to visit a friend. He planned on attending the inaugural Olympic Games only as a spectator. At the last minute, he entered the tennis competition. To his surprise, he won the gold medal with a 6–2, 6–2 victory over Egyptian Dionysios Kasdaglis in the final match. He also won the men's doubles with German partner Fredrich Traun. Boland served 18 years in the British parliament and was a strong voice for Irish independence.

10. **SEBASTIAN COE**

Sebastian Coe of Great Britain won the gold medals in the 1,500-meter race at the 1980 and 1984 Olympics. Following his celebrated track career, Coe was elected to the British parliament in 1992.

Olympic Tarzans

Bob Mathias had a brief career in the movies. The two-time Olympic decathlon champion portrayed himself in *The Bob Mathias Story* and starred opposite Jayne Mansfield in *It Happened in Athens,* a film about the 1896 Olympic marathon. While Mathias never approached his Olympic glory in the movies, he is one of several athletes who parlayed athletic success into a film career.

1. SONJA HENIE

Sonja Henie was the only female skater to win gold medals in three consecutive Olympic Games. The Norwegian won the event in 1928, 1932, and 1936. Captivated by her appeal, Twentieth Century-Fox head Darryl F. Zanuck signed Henie to a film contract. Her films combined romance and skating. Henie's first film, *One in a Million,* was a box-office smash. By 1938, she was earning $16,000 per week, making her the highest-paid Hollywood star. The next year, Henie ranked as the number-three box-office attraction. She was linked romantically with several of her leading men, including Tyrone Power. Briefly, she was engaged to pianist

Liberace. The novelty of the skating movie soon wore off, and, by the 1940s, her film career was over. A shrewd business-woman, Henie earned millions as an actress and as the featured performer in touring ice shows. When she died in 1969, her estate was valued at nearly $50 million.

2. JOHNNY WEISSMÜLLER

Johnny Weissmüller was one of the greatest athletic successes of all time. Between 1921 and 1929, the swimmer did not lose a race and set 67 world records during his career. Weissmüller won three gold medals at the 1924 Olympics in Paris and added two more four years later in Amsterdam. Hollywood producers spotted a photo of Weissmüller in an underwear advertisement. Realizing that the muscular swimmer would make a perfect screen Tarzan, MGM signed him to star in *Tarzan, the Ape Man* in 1932. He portrayed Tarzan in a dozen films between 1932 and 1948. Weissmüller also starred as Jungle Jim in a series of films during the 1950s. From 1933 to 1938, he was married to actress Lupe Velez.

3. BUSTER CRABBE

Johnny Weissmüller was not the only swimming star to portray Tarzan in the movies. Clarence "Buster" Crabbe won the gold medal in the 400-meter freestyle at the 1932 Los Angeles Olympics. Paramount Studios signed Crabbe to compete against Weissmüller at MGM. In Crabbe's first film, *King of the Jungle,* he portrayed Kaspa the Lion Man. In 1933, he played the title character in *Tarzan the Fearless.* Crabbe is best-known as the star of movie serials about Buck Rogers and Flash Gordon.

4. **HERMAN BRIX**

American Herman Brix won a silver medal in the shot put at the 1928 Amsterdam Olympics. Brix became an actor and changed his name to Bruce Bennett. He appeared in more than 100 films during a career that spanned 30 years. Bennett played Tarzan in several films, including *The New Adventures of Tarzan* and *Tarzan in Guatemala.* He also acted in the Humphrey Bogart classic *The Treasure of the Sierra Madre.*

5. **GLENN MORRIS**

In 1936, Glenn Morris of the United States won the decathlon at the Berlin Olympics. His notoriety led to a brief film career. His most notable film, *Tarzan's Revenge,* costarred swimming gold medalist Eleanor Holm.

6. **DON BRAGG**

The winner of the pole vault at the 1960 Rome Olympics, Don Bragg celebrated his victory by letting out a Tarzan yell. His ambition to portray Tarzan in the movies appeared to have been realized when he signed to star in the film *Tarzan and the Jewels of Opar* in 1964. Unfortunately, the film was not completed because of a lawsuit involving copyright infringement.

7. **HAROLD SAKATA**

Weightlifter Harold Sakata of the United States won the silver medal in the light heavyweight division at the 1948 Olympic Games. Following a successful career as a professional wrestler, Sakata embarked on an acting career. His most remarkable role was as Oddjob, a villain in the James Bond film *Goldfinger.*

8. VERA HRUBA

Czech figure skater Vera Hruba finished seventeenth at the 1936 Winter Olympics at Garmisch-Partenkirchen, Germany. The event was won by Sonja Henie. Like Henie, Hruba went on to a successful film career. She married Herbert Yates, head of Republic Studios. Using the screen name Vera Hruba Ralston, she starred in many B-movies, including *The Lady and the Monster.*

9. CAROL HEISS

American figure skater Carol Heiss won the silver medal in 1956 and the gold in the 1960 Squaw Valley Winter Olympics. Her film career stalled after her first film, *Snow White and the Three Stooges,* proved to be a disappointment at the box office.

10. NAT PENDLETON

Before he became an actor, Nat Pendleton won a silver medal in the super-heavyweight freestyle wrestling division at the 1920 Antwerp Olympics. Pendleton appeared in more than 100 films, including *The Thin Man.*

Other Claims to Fame

John Jacob Astor and Jay Gould, sons of two of America's richest men, won gold medals at the 1908 Olympics in London. Gould, son of the notorious robber baron Jay Gould, won a gold medal in the *jeu de paume* event, a form of court tennis. Astor, whose father perished on the *Titanic,* won his gold medal in the men's doubles of rackets, a game similar to squash. This section features Olympic athletes who went on to fame in other endeavors.

1. GEORGE PATTON

The modern pentathlon event at the 1912 Stockholm Olympics was dominated by Swedish athletes. Six of the top seven finishers were Swedes. The exception was American army lieutenant George Patton. The pentathlon consisted of five events—shooting, swimming, fencing, horseback riding, and running. Patton's consistency in all the events made him a threat to win a medal. In the shooting competition, he missed the target on one of his shots. Patton contended that in fact the bullet had gone through a hole made by one of his previous shots. Officials disagreed and dropped him to fifth place. If his shot had hit the target, he would have won the gold medal. During World War II, General Patton was commander of the Third Army. His flamboyant leadership helped achieve victory in Europe.

2. BENJAMIN SPOCK

Benjamin Spock was a member of the victorious American crew in the eight-oared-shell-with-coxswain rowing event at the 1924 Paris Olympics. Twenty-one years after winning his gold medal, Spock authored *The Common Sense Book of Baby and Child Care.* The book has sold nearly 50 million copies, making it one of the best-selling books in history. In 1972, Spock ran for president on the ticket of The People's Party and received nearly 80,000 votes.

3. ALFRED KRUPP

Alfred Krupp won a bronze medal as a member of the German eight-meter sailing crew at the 1936 Berlin Olympics. During World War II, Krupp owned an armaments works that supplied weapons for Adolf Hitler's armies. Following the Nazis' surrender, in 1945, Krupp was convicted as a war criminal at the Nuremberg trials.

4. RENÉ LACOSTE

During the 1924 Paris Olympics, French tennis player René Lacoste teamed with Jean Borotra to win a bronze medal in men's doubles. Lacoste later founded a famed clothing line.

5. JAMES CONNOLLY

The winner of the hop, step, and jump (triple jump) at the 1896 Athens Olympics was American James Connolly. Following his athletic career, Connolly wrote 25 novels and published hundreds of short stories and articles.

6. JEAN-JOSEPH RENAUD

Jean-Joseph Renaud was a member of the French sabre team that finished fourth at the 1908 Olympics. Renaud authored more than 60 novels during his literary career.

7. DOLLY GRAY

Clifford "Dolly" Gray won gold medals as a member of the American four-man bobsled team at the 1928 and 1932 Winter Olympics. A prolific songwriter, Gray wrote more than 3,000 songs.

8. JACK KELLY

Jack Kelly won a gold medal in the 1920 single sculls and double sculls rowing events. Four years later in Paris, he and partner Paul Costello prevailed again in the double sculls. Kelly's son, John, won a bronze medal in the 1956 single sculls. Kelly's daughter, Grace, was an Academy Award winning actress who later became Princess Grace of Monaco.

9. JACKSON SCHOLZ

Jackson Scholz outran fellow American Charley Paddock to win the gold medal in the 200-meter sprint at the 1924 Olympics. Scholz wrote more than 30 novels with sports subjects.

10. ALFRED GILBERT

Alfred Gilbert and Edward Cooke were co-winners of the pole vault at the 1908 Olympics. The two Americans both cleared a height of 12 feet, 2 inches. Gilbert invented the Erector set, a toy that has been a favorite of children for generations.

Going for the Gold

The speed and power of Olympic athletes make them excellent prospects for football. More than a dozen gold-medal winners have starred on the gridiron. Jim Hines, the gold medalist in the 100-meter dash at the 1968 Mexico City Olympics, played wide receiver for the Miami Dolphins and Kansas City Chiefs in 1969 and 1970. Gerald Tinker, a gold medalist in the 4×100-meter relay at the 1972 Munich Olympics, played wide receiver for the Atlanta Falcons and the Green Bay Packers. Glenn Davis, who won gold medals in the 400-meter hurdles at both the 1956 and 1960 Olympics, played two seasons as wide receiver with the Detroit Lions.

1. JIM THORPE

A gold medalist in both the decathlon and pentathlon at the 1912 Olympics, Jim Thorpe was also outstanding at football and baseball. Thorpe played major league baseball for the New York Giants for six years. In addition, Thorpe was an All-American at Carlisle College and starred in the National Football League from 1920 to 1928. Thorpe was elected to the Pro Football Hall of Fame in 1963.

2. BOB HAYES

Bob Hayes won the gold medal in the 100-meter dash at the 1964 Tokyo Olympics. Hayes used his blazing speed to become one of the NFL's most feared resources. He caught 371 passes and scored 76 touchdowns during his pro career with the Dallas Cowboys and the San Francisco Forty-Niners.

3. BOB MATHIAS

The decathlon champion in 1948 and 1952, Bob Mathias played fullback for Stanford in the 1952 Rose Bowl against Illinois. In a game against the University of Southern California, Mathias broke away for a 96-yard kickoff return.

4. JOHNNY LAM JONES

Johnny Lam Jones won his gold medal as a member of the American 4×100-meter relay at the 1976 Montreal Olympic Games. Jones played wide receiver for the New York Jets from 1980 to 1984. He caught 138 passes and scored 13 touchdowns.

5. RON BROWN

Another speedy wide receiver, Ron Brown won a gold medal as a member of the 1984 American 4×100-meter relay team. Brown caught 98 passes and scored 13 touchdowns during his NFL career with the Los Angeles Rams from 1984 to 1991.

6. JIM BAUSCH

The 1932 decathlon champion, Jim Bausch played professional football for Cincinnati and Chicago in 1933. The versatile Bausch played tailback, defensive back, and linebacker.

Before Michael Johnson, there was Bob Hayes. The gold medalist in the men's 100-meter dash at the 1964 Olympics was known then as "The World's Fastest Human."

7. GLENN MORRIS

Glenn Morris, the 1936 decathlon gold medalist, also played in the NFL. Morris played end for the Detroit Lions in 1940.

8. MILT CAMPBELL

Milt Campbell was the gold medalist in the decathlon at the 1956 Melbourne Olympics. He played halfback for the Cleveland Browns in 1957.

9. TOMMIE SMITH

The 200-meter-dash gold medalist at the 1968 Mexico City Olympics, Smith played briefly with the Cincinnati Bengals in 1969. Smith caught one pass, a 41-yard touchdown reception, but he was injured on the play and never caught another pass.

10. HENRY CARR

Like Tommie Smith, Henry Carr was a 200-meter champion. Carr won his gold medal at the 1964 Olympics. A defensive back for the New York Giants from 1965 to 1967, Carr intercepted seven passes.

Basket Cases

H ere are some of the Olympics' most memorable basket-ball moments.

1. 1972 GOLD-MEDAL GAME

The United States basketball team carried a 62-game winning streak into its gold-medal game against the Soviet Union in 1972. The Americans had won the gold medal in seven consecutive Olympics. Guard Doug Collins sank two free throws with three seconds remaining to give the United States a 50–49 lead. It appeared that the Americans had once again prevailed when the Soviets inbounded the ball but were unable to score before time expired.

Vladimir Kondrashkin, the Soviet coach, claimed he had called a time-out. The secretary-general of the International Basketball Association instructed the officials to reset the clock even though he did not have the authority to make the decision. Given another chance, Sasha Belov caught a length-of-the-court pass and made a lay-up at the buzzer to give the Soviet Union a shocking 51–50 victory. The American players, believing they were cheated out of the gold medal, refused to accept their silver medals.

2. **1936 GOLD-MEDAL GAME**

The first Olympic basketball competition occurred at the 1936 Berlin Olympics. Incredibly, the games were played outdoors on courts made of sand and clay. A downpour on the day of the game turned the courts to mud. The championship game was between the United States and Canada. Players had difficulty holding on to the slippery ball, and dribbling and shooting were nearly impossible. The United States won the gold medal with a 19–8 victory.

3. **ALFREDO RODRIGUES DA MOTTA**

Brazil and Mexico played in the 1948 bronze-medal game. Brazilian player Alfredo Rodrigues da Motta lost his shorts during the game and ran to the dressing room for a change. His team went on to win 52–47.

4. **BOB KURLAND**

The 1948 United States basketball team easily won the gold medal. Its average winning margin was more than 33 points per game. The team's star player was seven-foot center Bob Kurland. A tiny Chinese player discovered a unique way to get around the big center. He dribbled between Kurland's legs and made a lay-up.

5. **1952 GOLD-MEDAL GAME**

The basketball championship game of the 1952 Melbourne Olympics matched the United States and the Soviet Union. In the first half, the underdog Soviets slowed down play to keep the game close. Late in the game, the Americans decided to stall to protect their lead. As the action ground to a halt, a Soviet player sat on the floor in disgust. Although they shot only 20 percent for the game, the Americans won 36–25.

6. INTERNATIONAL BASKETBALL FEDERATION

Prior to the 1936 Olympic basketball competition, The International Basketball Federation passed a rule that banned all players taller than 6'3". Immediately, the United States, which would have had to replace three players, filed a protest. The IBF came to its senses and overturned the height rule.

7. HIRAM COLLEGE

Basketball did not become a medal sport until 1936. At the 1904 Olympics in St. Louis, basketball made its first appearance as an exhibition sport. Known as the Olympic World's College Basketball Championship, the exhibition included three American teams: Hiram College, Wheaton College, and the Latter Day Saints College (today known as Brigham Young University). Hiram defeated Wheaton 25–20 and the Latter Day Saints College 25–18 to win the competition.

8. IRAQ

The 1948 Iraqi basketball team was probably the worst in Olympic history. Its average losing margin was more than 80 points per game. Twice, to China and Korea, Iraq lost games by more than 100 points.

9. THE DREAM TEAM

In April 1989, the International Amateur Basketball Federation voted 56-13 to permit NBA players to compete in the Olympics. Incredibly, the United States voted against the proposal. The belief was that the lopsided games might hurt television ratings and fundraising efforts. The 1992 American squad, known as the Dream Team, was one of the greatest ever assembled. Superstars on the team included

Michael Jordan, Larry Bird, Magic Johnson, Karl Malone, John Stockton, Charles Barkley, Scottie Pippen, Patrick Ewing, David Robinson, and Clyde Drexler. As expected, the Dream Team won the gold medal. The Americans averaged 117 points per game with an average winning margin of 43 points.

10. UNIVERSAL STUDIOS

At the 1936 Olympic trials, a tournament was held to decide which basketball team would represent the United States. A team from Universal Studios won the trials and went on to win the gold medal.

Clothes Encounters

A thletes competed nude in the ancient Olympic Games. The modern Games have had their share of memorable attire. Australian Herb Elliott, the 1960 gold medalist in the 1,500-meter run, wore kangaroo-hide track shoes. Michael Johnson, winner of the 200- and 400-meter races at the 1996 Olympics, wore gold shoes to match the color of his medals.

1. FÉLIX CARBAJAL

Marathon runner Félix Carbajal's journey to the Olympics was almost as eventful as his race. The Cuban lost all of his money in a craps game in New Orleans and was forced to hitchhike to St. Louis for the 1904 Games. He arrived at the starting line wearing heavy shoes, long pants, and a long-sleeved shirt, an outfit not suited for a 26-mile race in 90-degree heat. American weightlifter Martin Sheridan came to his aid and cut off his pants legs and shirtsleeves. During the race, Carbajal worked up an appetite and stopped to eat green apples from an orchard along the marathon route. Not surprisingly, the green apples gave him stomach cramps. Despite the cramps, Carbajal finished a respectable fourth.

2. FROMENT-MEURICE

Women's golf was an Olympic event for the first and last time at the 1900 Paris Olympics. The French golfers handicapped themselves by wearing tight skirts and high heels. While they may have looked chic, the Frenchwomen were unable to win a medal. The top French finisher was a woman named Froment-Meurice, who shot 56 for nine holes to finish fourth.

3. KATARINA WITT

German figure skater Katarina Witt caused a stir with a revealing outfit in the short program at the 1988 Winter Olympics. Witt, already known for her sex appeal, wore a blue sequined outfit that was cut high in the thigh. Her principal rival, American Debi Thomas, remarked that Witt's costumes "belonged in an X-rated movie." Pressured by officials, Witt agreed to add a few feathers, much to the relief of her competitors and to the chagrin of her male admirers. Witt won the gold medal while Thomas settled for the bronze.

4. HASSIBA BOULMERKA

When Algerian middle-distance runner Hassiba Boulmerka trained on the roads of her own country, men often threw stones or spit on her. The reason for their contempt was that fundamentalist Muslims thought it shameful for a woman to run with bare legs in front of men. In their society, it is the custom for women to be covered from head to toe. Boulmerka persevered and won the gold medal in the 1,500-meter run at the 1992 Barcelona Games.

5. **DAVE WOTTLE**

American Dave Wottle wore a golf cap while he ran. Entering the final turn of the 1,500-meter race at the 1972 Olympics, Wottle was in sixth place. He unleashed a furious kick to break the tape just ahead of Yevhen Arzhanov of the Soviet Union. Wottle was so excited about his dramatic victory that he forgot to remove his hat on the medal stand during the playing of "The Star Spangled Banner." He later apologized to the American people, making it clear that he meant no disrespect.

6. **SONJA HENIE**

Sonja Henie won the gold medal in women's figure skating in 1928, 1932, and 1936. Her father, Wilhelm, was the owner of the largest furrier company in Norway. Rather than have his daughter wear the drab ankle-length skirts worn by other competitors, he insisted that she wear short skirts to catch the eye of the judges. Even in practice Henie wore spectacular outfits.

7. **PIETRO MENNEA**

Before a heat for the 200-meter dash at the 1972 Munich Olympics, Italian Pietro Mennea stripped down to his jockstrap while changing his shorts in the middle of the track. Mennea won the bronze medal at Munich but captured the gold eight years later in Moscow.

8. **ABEBE BIKILA**

Just prior to the 1960 marathon in Rome, Ethiopian runner Abebe Bikila wore out his favorite running shoes. He discovered that his new shoes pinched his feet. Fearful of developing blisters, Bikila decided to run the race barefooted.

Without shoes, Bikila still managed to win. Four years later in Tokyo, Bikila again won the gold medal, this time wearing shoes.

9. JOHN EISELE

At the 1908 Summer Olympics, American John Eisele wore white shorts as he prepared to run in the 3,200-meter steeplechase event. He was in violation of the rules that competitors must wear dark shorts. Facing disqualification, Eisele changed to dark shorts and went on to win the bronze medal.

10. JOIE RAY

Joie Ray of the United States finished fifth in the 1928 men's marathon. His feet were so swollen after the race that his track shoes had to be cut off.

The One and Only

These are one-of-a-kind Olympic feats.

1. EDDIE EAGAN

Eddie Eagan is the only athlete to win gold medals in both the Summer and Winter Olympics. In 1920, the American won a gold medal in the light heavyweight boxing division at the Antwerp Summer Olympics. Twelve years later, at the Lake Placid Winter Olympics, Eagan won another gold in the four-man bobsled competition.

2. OLIVER KIRK

The only boxer to win gold medals in two weight divisions in the same Olympics was American Oliver Kirk. At the 1904 St. Louis Games, he won gold medals in both the bantamweight and featherweight divisions.

3. 1908 BOXING COMPETITION

In 1908, for the only time in Olympic history, all the boxing matches were fought in a single day. Englishman Frederick

Spiller, the lightweight silver medalist, and Australian Reginald Baker, the silver medalist in the middleweight division, were required to fight four times that day.

4. ALVIN KRAENZLEIN

Alvin Kraenzlein of the United States is the only athlete to win four gold medals in individual track and field events at a single Olympic Games. At the 1900 Paris Olympics, Kraenzlein won the 60-meter dash, 110- and 200-meter hurdles, and the long jump.

5. ETHELDA BLEIBTREY

The only swimmer to win gold medals in all the events at an Olympics was American Ethelda Bleibtrey. She won gold medals in the 100-meter freestyle, 400-meter freestyle, and 4×100-meter relay, the only three swimming races for women at the 1920 Antwerp Olympics.

6. HELEN WAINWRIGHT

The only Olympic athlete to win medals in both swimming and diving was American Helen Wainwright. She won a silver medal in 1920 in the three-meter springboard diving competition and another silver medal in the 400-meter freestyle swimming race at the 1924 Paris Games.

7. LOTTIE DOD

Charlotte "Lottie" Dod is the only person to win a medal in Olympic archery and win five Wimbledon tennis titles. Dod won a silver medal in archery at the 1908 London Olympics. The Englishwoman won five Wimbledon singles titles between 1887 and 1893.

8. ÉTIENNE DESMARTEAU

American athletes won 21 of the 22 track and field events held at the 1904 Olympics in St. Louis. The only non-American to win a gold medal in track and field was Canadian Étienne Desmarteau, who won the 56-pound weight throw.

9. PETE RADEMACHER

Pete Rademacher won the gold medal in the superheavy-weight boxing division at the 1956 Melbourne Olympics. On August 22, 1957, Rademacher became the first and only Olympic gold medalist to fight for the heavyweight championship in his first professional fight. He floored champion Floyd Patterson in the second round but was stopped in the sixth round.

10. ROBERT WILLIAMS

The only Olympic gold medalist to have fought in the Civil War was Robert Williams. Williams won his gold medal in the team archery competition at the 1904 Olympics. Williams fought in a number of important battles, including Shiloh and Vicksburg.

Notable Nicknames

H elen Stephens, the 1936 100-meter-dash champion, was nicknamed The Fulton Flash. The 1960 100-meter gold medalist, Wilma Rudolph, was called The Black Gazelle because of her graceful stride. Here are ten more Olympic athletes with memorable nicknames.

1. THE SASKATOON LILY

Canadian high jumper Ethel Catherwood was nicknamed The Saskatoon Lily by a reporter who was beguiled by her exceptional beauty. Catherwood became one of the most popular athletes at the 1928 Amsterdam Olympics when she won the gold medal in the high jump. Exceptionally shy, she despised publicity of any kind. When it was suggested that she go to Hollywood to become an actress, Catherwood replied, "I'd rather gulp poison than try my hand at motion pictures."

2. MADAM BUTTERFLY

Swimmer Mary T. Meagher was so dominant in her specialty that she was dubbed Madam Butterfly. The 15-year-old

American won gold medals in the 100- and 200-meter butter-fly events at the 1984 Los Angeles Olympics.

3. THE VAULTING VICAR

Bob Richards won gold medals in the pole vault at the 1952 and 1956 Olympics. He was called The Vaulting Vicar because he was a minister of the Church of the Brethren.

4. THE WORLD'S FASTEST HUMAN

Charley Paddock lived up to his nickname as The World's Fastest Human by winning the gold medal in the 100-meter sprint at the 1920 Olympics. Paddock was famous for his flying finish. At the end of a race, he would leap into the tape with his arms extended in a V-formation.

5. THE ALBATROSS

At 6'7", German Michael Gross was one of the tallest swimmers ever to compete in the Olympics. With an armspan of more than seven feet, Gross was nicknamed The Albatross. Rather than having an albatross around his neck, Gross wore two gold medals. He won gold in the 100-meter butterfly and 200-meter freestyle at the 1984 Olympics.

6. THE THORPEDO

Australian swimming sensation Ian Thorpe is known as The Thorpedo because of the effortless way he cuts through the water. Thorpe won three gold medals at the 2000 Sydney Olympics.

7. BLACK HERCULES

John Davis was nicknamed The Black Hercules because of his extraordinary strength. Undefeated from 1938 to 1953,

Davis won gold medals in the 1948 and 1952 Olympics in the super heavyweight weightlifting competition.

8. THE FLYING FINN

The first of the great Finnish runners, Hannes Kolehmainen won gold medals in the 5,000- and 10,000-meter races at the 1912 Olympics. The Flying Finn also won the 1920 marathon.

9. THE MILWAUKEE METEOR

The Milwaukee Meteor, Archie Hahn, earned three gold medals in the 1904 Olympics. The sprinter won the 60-meter, 100-meter, and 200-meter races.

10. THE FLYING COP

New York City policeman Robert McAllister finished sixth in the 100-meter dash at the 1928 Amsterdam Olympics. McAllister, known as The Flying Cop, lost all chance for a medal when he pulled a tendon late in the race.

The Eagle Has Landed

N ot every nickname is a winner.

1. EDDIE THE EAGLE

Eddie Edwards was not your typical ski jumper. He came from England, a country not known for producing ski jumpers. Edwards hardly looked like an Olympic athlete. The 24-year-old plasterer from Cheltenham wore thick glasses. At the 1988 Winter Olympics, he had to borrow skis from the Austrians, a suit from the Germans, and a helmet from the Italians. The unlikely competitor was given the nickname Eddie the Eagle. Edwards finished last in both the 70- and 90-meter jump. On his best jump, he soared 180 feet, 114 feet short of the winning jump by Finland's Matti Nykanen. Admitting that he was terrified before each jump, Edwards said, "The most important thing was to survive."

2. CRASH

Nash McCrea was nicknamed Crash for good reason. During the five-mile cycling race at the 1904 Olympics, the American turned the event into a demolition derby. In one crash, McCrea took out Marcus Hurley and Burton Downing, American teammates who won gold medals in the one- and two-mile races. In another mishap, he swerved and caused a chain reaction that felled several more cyclists. American Charles Schlee survived the carnage to win the gold medal.

3. THE BEAST OF PRAGUE

One of the most successful distance runners in Olympic history, Emil Zátopek of Czechoslovakia always looked as if he were about to collapse. As one sportswriter put it, "He looked as though his neck was in a noose." Another reporter observed that Zátopek "looks as though he was stabbed in the heart." Zátopek was nicknamed The Beast of Prague because he always grimaced while running. He explained, "I was not talented enough to run and smile at the same time."

4. UNBEATABLE

Olympic boxing judging has always been controversial, but never more so than in the case of Korean Park Si-hun. At the 1988 Olympics in Seoul, South Korea, he won the gold medal in the light middleweight division with a little help from dubious judging. During the competition, he won a series of decisions that left opponents outraged and observers shaking their heads. In the gold-medal bout, Park defeated American Roy Jones, one of the best boxers of his generation, even though Jones landed more than twice as many punches. Embarrassed, officials named Jones the outstanding boxer in the Olympics. Park was given the gold medal and the nickname Unbeatable. The outrageous decision forced the International Boxing Federation to institute a new computerized scoring system to register punches landed.

5. THE SEAWEED STREAK

Australian swimmer Murray Rose won gold medals in the 400-meter freestyle events at the 1956 and 1960 Olympics. A strict vegetarian, Rose was nicknamed The Seaweed Streak.

6. THE SWEDISH STURGEON

Arne Borg of Sweden won the gold medal in the 1,500-meter freestyle swimming race at the 1928 Amsterdam Olympics. Borg was given the nickname The Swedish Sturgeon because he swam as naturally as a fish.

7. THE HUMAN FROG

Ray Ewry won a record ten gold medals in the standing jump events at the Olympics between 1900 and 1908. His ability to spring from a crouched position earned him the nickname The Human Frog.

8. THE QUIETLY CONFIDENT QUARTET

Until the 1980 Moscow Olympics, the American swimmers had won every gold medal in the 4×100-meter relay. With the Americans absent because of a boycott, the Australians became the favorites. The Australian team consisted of Mark Kerry, Peter Evans, Mark Tonelli, and Neil Brooks. They nicknamed themselves The Quietly Confident Quartet and edged the Soviets for the gold medal.

9. **Snowy**

Reginald Baker of Australia won a silver medal in the middle-weight boxing division at the 1908 London Olympics. An all-around athlete, Baker also competed in diving and swimming Olympic events. He was nicknamed Snowy because of his snow-white hair. In 1908, Baker was scheduled to referee the Tommy Burns–Jack Johnson heavyweight championship fight, but he was replaced when Johnson objected to the color of his hair.

10. **BONES**

Harrison Dillard was nicknamed Bones because he was so thin. Dillard won gold medals in the 100-meter dash at the 1948 Olympics and in his specialty, the 100-meter hurdles, at the 1952 Helsinki Games.

Olympic Names

Each of these athletes had names that made them naturals for the Olympics.

1. LEWIS MOIST

Although he was eliminated in the semifinals of the 1,500-meter freestyle swimming race at the 1908 London Olympics, British swimmer Lewis Moist certainly had the best name.

2. JEFF FLOAT

Swimmer Jeff Float won a gold medal as part of the American 4×200-meter freestyle relay team at the 1984 Los Angeles Olympics.

3. DAVID FALL

David Fall won a silver medal in platform diving at the 1924 Paris Olympics. The gold medal was won by fellow American Albert White.

4. ERNST FAST

Ernst Fast of Sweden finished third in the marathon at the 1900 Paris Olympics. While he was fast, he was not fast enough, finishing 37 minutes behind winner Michel Théato of Luxembourg.

5. ÉMILE CHAMPION

Émile Champion of France nearly lived up to his name in the 1900 marathon. Champion finished second behind Michel Théato.

6. ALFRED SWIFT

South African cyclist Alfred Swift won a bronze medal in the 1,000-meter time trial at the 1956 Melbourne Olympics. Italian Leandro Faggin was swifter than Swift and won the gold medal.

7. SHANE GOULD

Swimming sensation Shane Gould won three gold medals at the 1972 Munich Olympics. She proved the old adage, "All that glitters is Gould."

8. LUZ LONG

Jesse Owens won the gold medal in the long jump at the 1936 Berlin Olympics. The silver medalist was a German with the perfect name for a long jumper, Luz Long.

9. FRANCIS LANE

In running events, each competitor is assigned a lane. At the 1896 Athens Olympics, American Francis Lane won a bronze medal in the 100-meter dash.

10. **WILLIAM PRESS**

A pinfall in wrestling is also known as a body press. William Press of Great Britain won a silver medal in the bantam-weight division of freestyle wrestling at the 1908 Olympics. Defeated in the gold-medal match by American George Mehnert, Press refused to shake hands.

name Games

If gold medals were given for names, these athletes would have stood on the podium.

1. MAN AFRAID SOAP

A Canadian team of Mohawk Indians won the bronze medal in lacrosse at the 1904 St. Louis Olympics. The players on the team had wonderful Indian names such as Half Moon, Almighty Voice, Spotted Tail, Snake Eater, Rain in Face, and Flat Iron. One player was named Man Afraid Soap, which makes you wonder how popular he was with his teammates after a tough lacrosse match.

2. WILLIAM BATHE

At the other extreme, there was a swimmer named William Bathe who competed in the 1912 Stockholm Olympics. Bathe won a gold medal in the 400-meter breaststroke.

3. WILHELMINA LUST

Wilhelmina Lust of Holland finished fifth in the 1952 women's long jump. Yvette Williams of New Zealand won the gold medal.

4. WILFRED LEGG

Wilfred Legg finished fifth in the 100-meter dash at the 1928 Amsterdam Olympics. The race was won by Percy Williams of Canada.

5. SUMMER SANDERS

One of the stars of the 1992 Summer Olympics was American swimmer Summer Sanders. She won a gold medal in the 200-meter butterfly and a silver medal in the 200-meter individual medley.

6. ERNST GOOD

Swiss skier Ernst Good won the silver medal in the giant slalom at the 1976 Winter Olympics in Innsbruck. While Ernst was good, teammate Heini Hemmi was better and won the gold.

7. SHIRLEY STRONG

Shirley Strong of Great Britain was the silver medalist in the 100-meter hurdles at the 1984 Los Angeles Olympics. American Benita Fitzgerald Brown defeated Strong by four-hundredths of a second.

8. BEN TRASH

Ben Trash of the United States finished fourth in the plain high-diving competition at the 1924 Paris Olympics. It was the last time that the high dive was an Olympic event.

9. LAJOS KISS

Lajos Kiss of Hungary won the bronze medal in the 1,000-meter kayak singles at the 1956 Melbourne Olympics.

10. **JAMES LUCK**

American James Luck finished fifth in the 400-meter hurdles at the 1964 Summer Olympics. Another American, Rex Cawley, won the gold medal.

Food for Thought

An ancient Olympian, Empedokles of Agrigentum cele-brated his victory by having an ox made of dough gar-nished with herbs and spices. He had the great ox cut into small pieces, which he gave to the spectators. The following Olympians also had food on their minds.

1. PAAVO NURMI

Finnish distance runners were known for their endurance. In the 1920s, newspapers started publishing far-fetched stories about how the Finns trained. It was said that they baked themselves in huts filled with hot rocks, then took ice baths followed by rolls in the snow. Paavo Nurmi, the great Finnish runner who won nine gold medals between 1920 and 1928, was asked by a naïve reporter if he subsisted on a diet of raw fish and black bread. Nurmi, perplexed by the question, replied that his favorite food was oatmeal.

2. THOMAS HAMILTON-BROWN

At the 1936 Berlin Olympics, South African lightweight boxer Thomas Hamilton-Brown lost a split decision to Carlos Lillo of Chile. Officials later discovered that there was an error in the scoring and that Hamilton-Brown had really won. But following the loss, he had stuffed himself with food and was unable to meet the weight limit for his next bout.

3. RAGNHILD HVEGER

Prior to the 400-meter freestyle event at the 1936 Olympics, Danish swimmer Ragnhild Hveger was presented with a box of chocolates by a friend. She gave the pieces of chocolate to the other swimmers in the final except her main rival, Hendrika Mastenbroek of Holland. Mastenbroek avenged the slight by winning the gold medal. Hveger settled for the silver.

4. DAWN FRASER

On the night before the 100-meter freestyle swimming event at the 1956 Melbourne Games, Australian Dawn Fraser had a nightmare. She dreamed that she was swimming in a pool of spaghetti. No matter how hard she stroked, she went nowhere. Luckily, the real race was in water, and Fraser set a world record and won the gold medal. Four years later, at the Rome Olympics, Fraser refused to swim the butterfly leg of the medley relay because she had eaten a huge plate of spaghetti and was too stuffed to compete.

5. HARRY HILLMAN

American Harry Hillman won gold medals in the 400-meter run and 400-meter hurdles at the 1904 Olympics. Hillman attributed his success to his unusual diet. He refrained from eating meat and sweets, but he did advocate swallowing whole eggs.

6. IVAR JOHANSSON

Swedish wrestler Ivar Johansson won the gold medal in the middleweight freestyle division at the 1932 Los Angeles

Dutch swimmer Hendrika Mastenbroek was called "The Empress of Berlin" at the 1936 Olympic games there.

Olympics. Following his victory, he fasted for four days and lost 11 pounds. Entering the welterweight division of Greco-Roman wrestling, Johansson again walked away with the gold medal.

7. NANCY GREENE

The coach of Canadian skier Nancy Greene came up with an ingenious way to keep her from being nervous before the giant slalom race at the 1968 Grenoble Winter Olympics. He suggested that she have a snack at a nearby restaurant. Just before the race began, he rushed Greene to the slopes. The unconventional approach worked, and Greene won the gold medal.

8. DEBBIE ARMSTRONG

American skier Debbie Armstrong had never won a World Cup race prior to the 1984 Sarajevo Winter Olympics. On the night before the giant slalom, Armstrong stayed up and ate peanut butter. The next day she shocked the skiing world by winning the gold medal.

9. JAMES CONNOLLY

The winner of the triple jump at the 1896 Olympics, American James Connolly raised the money to travel to Athens through bake sales.

10. NAOKO TAKAHASHI

Naoko Takahashi of Japan won the women's marathon at the 2000 Sydney Olympics. The slender runner admitted she had a weakness for buffets.

Drinking It All In

After Eugene-Henri Gravelotte of France won the foil event at the 1896 Athens Olympics, he celebrated his victory by drinking a glass of retzina wine at the Acropolis. During the running of the 1908 London marathon, American Johnny Hayes gargled with brandy and washed his face with Florida water on his way to the gold medal. In 1952, the Jamaican 4 × 400-meter relay runners celebrated their gold medal by drinking whiskey at the hotel with the Duke of Edinburgh. Frank Shorter, the gold medalist in the 1972 Munich marathon, celebrated by drinking three glasses of gin while bathing in a bathtub.

1. 1932 BRAZILIAN OLYMPIC TEAM

The Brazilian Olympic team arrived by boat in Los Angeles for the 1932 Summer Olympics. Strapped for cash, the athletes were forced to sell coffee brought from Brazil to cover their expenses. Many athletes never made it off the boat.

2. THOMAS HICKS

With ten miles left to run in the 1904 St. Louis marathon, American Thomas Hicks held a lead of more than a mile.

Exhausted, Hicks wanted to stop and rest. He was sponged down with water and given some brandy by his handlers. When he did not respond, they administered a potion made of egg whites laced with strychnine. The potentially lethal combination temporarily revived him, but by the time Hicks neared the end of the marathon, he was hallucinating. Near collapse, Hicks finished the race almost six minutes ahead of silver medalist Albert Coray for France.

3. ORLANDO PIETRI

Italian Orlando Pietri was leading the 1908 marathon in London when he staggered into the Olympic stadium. Disoriented, he collapsed several times and was disqualified for being aided by well-meaning spectators. It was thought that Pietri's collapse was caused by exhaustion. Years later, runner Joe Deakin came up with another possible explanation. He revealed that Pietri was given Chantilly, an alcoholic drink, by spectators during the race. Deaken suggested that Pietri had become tipsy.

4. JULES NOËL

Prohibition was still in effect when the 1932 Summer Olympics were staged in Los Angeles. Teams from France and Italy were permitted to bring bottles of wine for their athletes. During the discus event, Frenchman Jules Noël drank champagne between throws. Noël finished fourth, missing a medal by four inches.

5. GABRIELLA DORIO

Italian Gabriella Dorio won the gold medal in the women's 1,500-meter run at the 1984 Los Angeles Olympics. To celebrate, she took a bath in wine.

6. ALBIN LERMUSIAUX

In the first Olympic marathon in 1896, Frenchman Albin Lermusiaux led for most of the 26-mile race. At just past the halfway mark, Lermusiaux was given an alcoholic rubdown by supporters. He appeared on his way to victory when he accepted a glass of wine from a spectator. Almost immediately, he began to feel the effects from the alcohol on his dehydrated system, and he collapsed with six miles left in the race. Spiridon Louis of Greece won the gold medal.

7. CHARLES HEFFERON

Charles Hefferon learned the hard way that you should drink champagne after a victory and not before. The South African led the 1908 marathon with just two miles remaining when he foolishly accepted a drink of champagne. He reacted badly to the alcohol and quickly developed stomach cramps. Although he relinquished the lead, he did manage to hold on for the silver medal.

8. JOSEPH GUILLEMOT

Joseph Guillemot of France had the misfortune of competing in many races with the great Paavo Nurmi. He rarely defeated his Finnish rival. Before the 5,000-meter race at the 1920 Antwerp Olympics, Guillemot was handed a mystery beverage by the French trainer. "Drink this and you'll be unbeatable," he was told. Filled with confidence, Guillemot defeated Nurmi for the gold medal. Later, Guillemot discovered that the magic elixir was merely a combination of rum, sugar, and water.

9. EGIL DANIELSEN

All Egil Danielsen needed was a good cup of coffee to help him win the gold medal in the javelin throw at the 1956

Melbourne Games. Another competitor, Michel Macquet of France, offered him a cup of coffee to help him calm his nerves. The Norwegian, who rarely drank coffee, broke the world record by 6 feet with a throw of 281 feet. Danielsen's mighty throw was more than 18 feet farther than that of silver medalist Janusz Sidlo of Poland.

10. JEAN-CLAUDE KILLY

French skier Jean-Claude Killy was the favorite to win the giant slalom at the 1968 Grenoble Winter Olympics. On the night before the race, the heater in Killy's room malfunctioned, causing the temperature to drop below freezing. As Killy shivered in bed, he heard a loud noise that resembled a gunshot. It turned out to be a bottle of champagne that exploded in the frigid temperature. Killy was so confident of victory that he had the champagne on hand for an expected celebration. Despite the uncomfortable evening, Killy won the gold medal in the giant slalom.

Bigger Is Better

These Olympians were larger than life.

1. CHRIS TAYLOR

Four-hundred-and-twelve-pound American Chris Taylor was one of the favorites in the super heavyweight division of freestyle wrestling at the 1972 Munich Olympics. The big man from Michigan lost a controversial decision to Oleksander Medvid of the Soviet Union when he was penalized for passivity. Taylor settled for the bronze medal. In the 1970s, Taylor was a popular professional wrestler. His weight as a professional ballooned to more than 450 pounds.

2. YAO MING

The Chinese basketball team did not win a medal at the 2000 Sydney Olympics, but they did boast the tournament's tallest player. Seven-foot, six-inch Yao Ming impressed NBA scouts with his shot-blocking ability.

3. ROMAN CODREANU

One of the largest men ever to compete in the Olympics, Romanian Roman Codreanu won a bronze medal in the super heavyweight division of Greco-Roman wrestling at the 1976 Montreal Olympics. Codreanu weighed more than 375 pounds.

4. MARK HENRY

At the 1992 Barcelona Olympics, American Mark Henry did not win a medal, but he did break the record as the heaviest weightlifter in Olympic history. The super heavyweight tipped the scales at 366 pounds. Henry later wrestled professionally as Sexual Chocolate. According to the storyline, the 400-pounder impregnated a 79-year-old woman wrestler named Mae Young.

5. PATRICK MCDONALD

Patrick McDonald was one of a group of large American track and field athletes known as The Whales. The 350-pound New York City policeman won gold medals in the shot put at the 1912 Stockholm Olympics and the 56-pound weight throw at the 1920 Antwerp games.

6. VASSILY ALEKSEYEV

Super heavyweight weightlifter Vassily Alekseyev of the Soviet Union won gold medals at the 1972 and 1976 Summer Olympics. The 350-pound strongman set nearly 80 world records during his career.

7. HITOSHI SAITO

Hitoshi Saito could throw his weight around and his opponent around as well. The 320-pound Japanese judo champion won the gold medals in the heavyweight division at the 1984 and 1988 Olympics.

8. HUMBERTO SELVETTI

Humberto Selvetti's weight actually cost him a gold medal. At the 1956 Olympics, the Argentine weightlifter tied American Paul Anderson for the most weight lifted. The two men each lifted 500 kilograms in the combined press, snatch, and jerk lifts. Anderson was awarded the gold medal because he weighed less, 304 pounds to Selvetti's 316.

9. PAEA WOLFGRAMM

Tonga is not known for its boxing champions. A major surprise at the 1996 Atlanta Olympics was Tongan super heavyweight Paea Wolfgramm's silver medal. The 310-pounder might have won the gold medal, but he had to fight his final match with a fractured wrist. He lost the decision to Vladimir Klichko of Ukraine.

10. CHERYL HAWORTH

Women's weightlifting was a medal sport for the first time at the 2000 Sydney Olympics. Seventeen-year-old American Cheryl Haworth won the bronze medal in the super heavyweight division. Haworth, who weighed 307 pounds, lifted 320 pounds in the clean-and-jerk category.

Small Packages

You do not have to be a giant to be an Olympic athlete.

1. UNKNOWN FRENCH BOY

One of the greatest mysteries in Olympic history was the identity of a French boy who helped win a gold medal in the paired-oared-shell-with-coxswain rowing race at the 1900 Paris Olympics. The Dutch team of Francois Brandt and Roelof Klein decided that their coxswain, Hermanus Brockmann, was too heavy and was slowing their boat down. Their solution was to ask a young French boy to serve as their coxswain. Despite the inexperienced coxswain, the team from Amsterdam won the gold medal. It was estimated that the boy was around ten years old and weighed approximately 70 pounds. His identity may forever remain a mystery. After the race, the youth disappeared before anyone learned his name.

2. AILEEN RIGGIN

Fourteen-year-old Aileen Riggin won the gold medal in platform diving at the 1920 Olympics. The 4′ 7″, 65-pound American was the smallest competitor at the Games.

3. JOE DI PIETRO

Mighty mite Joe Di Pietro won the gold medal in the bantam-weight weightlifting division at the 1948 London Olympics. The American stood just 4'8", and his arms were so short that he could barely lift the bar over his head.

4. MARY LOU RETTON

Mary Lou Retton was a 90-pound dynamo who electrified the gymnastic world with her performance at the 1984 Los Angeles Games. Retton scored perfect tens in the floor exercise and vault to win the gold medal in the women's all-around.

5. KERRI STRUG

Kerri Strug, an 85-pound American gymnast, displayed a huge amount of courage in the team combined exercises at the 1996 Atlanta Olympics. The 18-year-old injured her left ankle on a vault landing. Believing that she needed to get a better score to guarantee a gold medal for the American team, Strug scored 9.712 on her second vault. As it turned out, the Americans would have won anyway, but that did not diminish Strug's achievement.

6. CHARLES VINCI

Four-foot, ten-inch weightlifter Charles Vinci was almost disqualified because he was too big. At the 1956 Melbourne Olympics, the American discovered 15 minutes before the weigh-in that he was half a pound overweight. Frantically, Vinci thought of ways to instantly lose weight. He scraped dead skin off his feet and cut his hair. Miraculously, he made the 123-pound bantamweight limit. Vinci not only qualified for the event, he went on to win the gold medal.

Kerri Strug tries to stick her landing, despite her injured ankle, at the 1996 Atlanta Olympics.

7. ALEKSEI VAKHONIN

The winner of the gold medal in the bantamweight division of weightlifting at the 1964 Tokyo Games was Aleksei Vakhonin. The Russian was only 4' 10", making him one of the shortest gold medalists in Olympic history.

8. BILLY SHERRING

Canadian Billy Sherring won the marathon at the 1906 Athens Olympics by nearly seven minutes. When Sherring was weighed after the race, it was discovered that he had lost nearly 15 pounds. Billy Sherring weighed only 98 pounds, but he was certainly no weakling. If Sherring had been a Greek, he could have quickly regained the weight. Before the Games, local store owners promised the marathon winner a loaf of bread and three cups of coffee every day for a year plus a free lunch for six every Sunday, provided the gold medalist was from Greece.

9. OLGA KORBUT

The darling of the 1972 Munich Olympics, Soviet gymnast Olga Korbut won gold medals in the balance beam and floor exercise. The elfin-like Korbut stood 4' 11".

10. NADIA COMANECI

Fourteen-year-old gymnast Nadia Comaneci scored seven perfect tens at the 1976 Montreal Olympics. The 85-pound Romanian won gold medals in the uneven bars, balance beam, and all-around events.

Life Begins at Fifty

At the 1936 Berlin Olympics, 72-year-old Artur von Pongracz was a member of the Austrian equestrian team. He is just one of the many older athletes who competed in the Olympics.

1. OSCAR SWAHN

Sixty-year-old Oscar Swahn won a gold medal in the team running deer shooting, single-shot competition at the 1908 London Olympics. The objective was to hit a running deer target. Twelve years later, the 72-year-old bearded Swedish marksman won a silver medal in the team running deer, double-shot event. His son, Alfred, was also a member of both medal-winning teams.

2. SAMUEL DUVALL

Sixty-eight-year-old Samuel Duvall was a member of an American archery team that finished second at the 1904 St. Louis Olympics. The archers belonged to a Cincinnati archery club.

3. LOUIS NOVERRAZ

Louis Noverraz won a silver medal as a crew member for Switzerland in the 5.5-meter sailing competition at the 1968 Mexico City Olympics. Noverraz was 66 years old.

4. GALEN SPENCER

Sixty-four-year-old Galen Spencer was a member of the victorious United States archery team at the 1904 St. Louis Olympics. Spencer is the oldest American champion in Olympic history.

5. ROBERT WILLIAMS, JR.

American archers at the 1904 St. Louis Olympics were the oldest group of athletes in the Games' history. Robert Williams, Jr., who won a gold medal in the Double York Round, was 63 years old.

6. JOSHUA MILLNER

Sixty-one-year-old Joshua Millner won the gold medal in the free rifle shooting competition at the 1908 London Olympics. The target was 1,000 yards away. The Irishman had an unorthodox shooting technique. He lay on his back with his knees drawn up and the rifle supported by his feet.

7. BILL ROYCROFT

Bill Roycroft won a bronze medal as a member of the Australian team in the three-day equestrian competition at the 1976 Montreal Olympics. Roycroft was 61 years old when he won his medal. His son, Wayne, was also a member of the three-man team.

8. JOHN BUTT

John Butt was 61 years old when he won a silver medal as a member of the British trapshooting team at the 1912 Stockholm Olympics.

9. WILLIAM MILNE

John Butt was not the only 60-year-old British marksman who won a medal at the 1912 Olympic games. Sixty-year-old William Milne won a silver medal in the small-bore rifle, prone position competition.

10. MAX HOUBEN

The oldest medalist in Winter Olympic history was Belgian Max Houben. The 57-year-old won a silver medal in the four-man bobsled competition at the 1948 St. Moritz Olympics.

You're Never Too Young

Eleven-year-old figure skater Cecilia Colledge of Great Britain finished eighth at the 1932 Lake Placid Winter Olympics. Another 11-year-old, Carlos Front of Spain, competed as a coxswain in the coxswain-in-the-eights rowing competition at the 1992 Barcelona Games. Here are ten more young athletes who competed successfully in the Olympics.

1. DIMITRIOS LOUNDRAS

Ten-year-old Dimitrios Loundras of Greece finished third in the parallel-bars portion of the team gymnastic competition at the 1896 Athens Olympics. Loundras is the youngest athlete to finish in the top three at the Olympics.

2. LUIGINA GIAVOTTI

The Italian women's gymnastic team at the 1928 Amsterdam Olympics included three athletes who were 12 years old or younger. Luigina Giavotti was 11 years old, while teammates Ines Vercesi and Clara Marangoni were 12. Despite their youth, the Italians won a silver medal.

3. **MARJORIE GESTRING**

Thirteen-year-old American Marjorie Gestring won the gold medal in springboard diving at the 1936 Berlin Olympics. She is the youngest athlete in Summer Olympics history to win a gold medal in an individual event.

4. **FU MINGXIA**

The gold medalist in platform diving at the 1992 Olympics was 13-year-old Fu Mingxia of China. Four years later she repeated as Olympic champion.

5. **DOROTHY POYNTON**

Thirteen-year-old American Dorothy Poynton won a silver medal in springboard diving at the 1928 Olympics. She won gold medals in platform diving at the 1932 and 1936 games.

6. **NADIA COMANECI**

Romanian gymnast Nadia Comaneci won the gold medal in the all-around competition at the 1976 Montreal Olympics. After reaching the top of the gymnastic world, she was asked by a reporter if she had plans for retirement. Comaneci replied, "No, I'm only 14."

7. **KUSUO KITAMURA**

At the 1932 Los Angeles Olympics, 14-year-old Japanese swimmer Kusuo Kitamura won the gold medal in the 1,500-meter freestyle.

8. **SONJA HENIE**

Sonja Henie was 11 years old when she finished last in women's figure skating at the 1924 Olympics. Henie made history by winning the gold medal at the next three Winter Olympics.

9. ULRIKE MEYFARTH

In 1972, 16-year-old Ulrike Meyfarth won the women's long jump. The West German became the youngest athlete ever to win the gold medal in an individual track and field event. Meyfarth also won the long jump gold medal in 1984.

10. BILLY FISKE

Billy Fiske, a 16-year-old, won a gold medal as a member of the American four-man bobsled team at the 1928 St. Moritz Olympics. Fiske won a second gold medal in the four-man bobsled event in 1932.

Multi-Sport Medalists

Each of these athletes won medals in more than one Olympic event.

1. EDDIE EAGAN

American Eddie Eagan won a gold medal in the light heavyweight division at the 1920 Summer Olympics. In 1932, Eagan casually informed his wife, "Guess what? I'm on the American bobsled team." This came as a surprise since he had never been in a bobsled. The Americans won the gold medal at the Lake Placid Winter Olympics, and Eagan became the first athlete to win gold medals at both the Winter and Summer Olympics.

2. CHRISTA ROTHENBURGER

Christa Rothenburger of the German Democratic Republic won gold medals in the 500-meter speed-skating competition at the 1984 Sarajevo Winter Olympics and in the 1,000-meter speed skating at the 1988 Calgary Games. At the 1988 Seoul Summer Olympics, Rothenburger won a silver medal in the 1,000-meter match sprint-cycling competition.

3. JACOB TULLIN THAMS

Jacob Tullin Thams of Norway won a gold medal in the 90-meter ski jumping competition at the 1924 Chamonix Winter Olympics. At the 1936 Berlin Summer Games, Thams earned a silver medal as a member of the Norwegian crew in the eight-meter sailing competition.

4. VIGGO JENSEN

Denmark's Viggo Jensen won the gold medal in the super heavyweight weightlifting competition at the 1896 Athens Olympics. Jensen also finished second in the free pistol-shooting competition and third in the military rifle.

5. CARL SCHUHMANN

One of the most versatile athletes in Olympic history was German Carl Schuhmann. He won the super heavyweight Greco-Roman wrestling competition at the 1896 Athens Olympics. Schuhmann also won the long horse vault gymnastic event. The multitalented athlete also competed in the long jump, triple jump, and shot put.

6. FRANK KUNGLER

American Frank Kungler won the silver medal in the heavyweight division of freestyle wrestling at the 1904 St. Louis Olympics. Kungler also finished third in the all-around dumbbell contest weightlifting event and in the tug-of-war team competition.

7. EDWIN FLACK

Australian Edwin Flack won the 800- and 1,500-meter races at the 1896 Athens Olympics. Although he had never before run in a marathon, he led with two miles to go before dropping out of the race. Flack also competed in the tennis competition.

8. NIKOLAI PANIN

Skater Nikolai Panin won a special-figures competition at the 1908 London Olympics. Panin just missed another medal when he finished fourth in the 1912 shooting team competition.

9. FANNY BLANKERS-KOEN

Fanny Blankers-Koen was the sensation of the 1948 London Olympics. She won gold medals in the 100- and 200-meter dashes and in the 80-meter hurdles. She won a fourth gold medal in the 4×100-meter relay. The Dutch woman may also have won the high jump and long jump had she been allowed to enter. At that time, track and field athletes were limited to competing in three individual events.

10. TIM SHAW

World-class swimmers normally do not compete in water polo events, but Tim Shaw was an exception. The American won a silver medal in the 400-meter freestyle swimming competition at the 1976 Montreal Olympics. Shaw won another silver medal as a member of the United States water polo team at the Los Angeles Games in 1984.

Al Oerter won the discus competition at four consecutive Olympics between 1956 and 1968. Here he attempts a throw at Mexico City in 1968.

Three's a Charm

I n the sixth century B.C., Milon of Kroton won the wrestling competition at five consecutive Olympiads. In the modern Games, several athletes have won their event at three consecutive Olympics.

1. **AL OERTER**

Al Oerter won the discus competition at four consecutive Olympics between 1956 and 1968. The American won the 1964 event despite wearing a neck brace to protect a cervical disc injury. A week before the Tokyo Games, Oerter made his task even more difficult by tearing cartilage in his ribs. Despite his injuries, Oerter threw the discus 200 feet and one inch to set an Olympic record.

2. **CARL LEWIS**

Carl Lewis won nine gold medals, four of them in the long jump. Lewis won the long jump in 1984, 1988, 1992, and 1996.

3. PAUL ELVSTROM

Paul Elvstrom may not be the most famous Olympic athlete, but he is one of only three to win the same event at four consecutive Olympics. The Dane won the gold medal in the Finn class sailing competition in every Olympics from 1948 to 1960.

4. GILLIS GRAFSTRÖM

The only man to win three consecutive Olympic figure skating gold medals was Gillis Grafström of Sweden. He won the event in 1920, 1924, and 1928. The 38-year-old Grafström finished second in 1932.

5. TEÓFILO STEVENSON

Cuban boxer Teófilo Stevenson won three consecutive gold medals in the super heavyweight division. Stevenson, feared for his devastating right hand, was the Olympic champion in 1972, 1976, and 1980.

6. VIKTOR SANEYEV

Viktor Saneyev of the Soviet Union won the triple jump in 1968, 1972, and 1976. Saneyev won the silver medal at the 1980 Moscow Olympics.

7. KLAUS DIBIASI

Italian Klaus Dibiasi won the silver medal in platform diving at the 1964 Tokyo Olympics. Dibiasi won the gold medal in the same event in 1968, 1972, and 1976. At the Montreal Olympics, Dibiasi defeated American Greg Louganis, the 1984 and 1988 champion.

8. DAWN FRASER

Dawn Fraser of Australia dominated the 100-meter freestyle swimming competition in the Olympics from 1956 to 1964. Fraser set a world record in the event at the 1956 Melbourne Games and set Olympic records in Rome and Tokyo.

9. MARTIN SHERIDAN

Martin Sheridan won the gold medal in the discus at the 1904, 1906, and 1908 Olympics. Sheridan, one of the first American track and field stars, won five gold medals during his Olympic career.

10. FRANK WYKOFF

Sprinter Frank Wykoff won three consecutive gold medals in the 4×100-meter relay race. Wykoff was a member of the victorious American relay teams in 1928, 1932, and 1936. Although Jesse Owens, the hero of the Berlin Games, was a member of the winning 1936 team, Wykoff was selected to run the anchor leg.

Medal Masters

There have been many athletes who have won ten or more Olympic medals. Despite their success, many of them are not household names.

1. LARISA LATYNINA

Soviet gymnast Larisa Latynina holds the record for the most medals during an Olympic career. Latynina won 18 medals in gymnastics from 1956 to 1964. Nine of her medals were gold.

2. NIKOLAI ANDRIANOV

Nikolai Andrianov of the Soviet Union won the gold medal in the all-around gymnastic competition at the 1976 Montreal Olympics. Andrianov won 15 medals during his career: seven gold, five silver, and three bronze.

3. EDOARDO MANGIAROTTI

Italian fencer Edoardo Mangiarotti won 13 medals from 1952 to 1960. Mangiarotti won six gold medals: five in épée and one in foil.

4. BORIS SHAKHLIN

Ukrainian gymnast Boris Shakhlin won the gold medal in the all-around competition at the 1960 Rome Olympics. Shakhlin won seven medals at the 1960 games and 13 overall.

5. TAKASHI ONO

Takashi Ono won the gold medal in the horizontal bar at the 1956 and 1960 Olympics. The Japanese gymnast won 13 medals during his Olympic career.

6. PAAVO NURMI

The Finnish runner Paavo Nurmi won nine gold medals from 1920 to 1928. Overall, Nurmi won a dozen medals in Olympic competition.

7. SAWAO KATO

Sawao Kato of Japan won gold medals in the men's all-around gymnastic competitions at the 1968 and 1972 Olympics. Kato was the winner of twelve medals in competition, eight of them gold.

8. CARL OSBURN

Carl Osburn won a gold medal in the military rifle competition at the 1920 Antwerp Olympics. The American won 11 medals in shooting competitions.

9. VIKTOR CHUKARIN

The men's all-around Olympic gymnastic champion in 1952 and 1956, Viktor Chukarin of the Soviet Union won four gold medals at the Helsinki Games. Overall, Chukarin won 11 medals including seven gold medals.

10. **RAY EWRY**

The standing high jump, standing long jump, and standing triple jump were Olympic events from 1900 to 1912. American Ray Ewry won a record ten gold medals in standing jump competitions from 1900 to 1908.

Bob Beamon still holds the Olympic record with his 29 feet, 2 ½ inch long jump at the 1968 Mexico City Games.

Great Performances

These athletes provided some of the Olympics' most dominant performances.

1. BOB BEAMON

Bob Beamon was one of the favorites in the long jump at the 1968 Mexico City Olympics. His biggest challengers were the co-holders of the world record, American Ralph Boston and Igor Ter-Ovanesyan of the Soviet Union. On his first jump, Beamon soared nearly six feet into the air. When he landed at the far end of the jumping pit, it was apparent that he had set a new world record. Beamon's incredible leap of 29 feet, 2 ½ inches broke the world record by 22 inches, and he won the gold medal by nearly two-and-a-half feet. The American was so overwhelmed by his achievement that he suffered a cataplectic seizure and collapsed on the track.

2. MICHAEL JOHNSON

At the 1996 Atlanta Olympics, American sprinter Michael Johnson ran the fastest race ever by a human being. Johnson was timed in the 200-meter dash at 19.32 seconds, breaking his own world record by .34 seconds.

3. 1924 CANADIAN HOCKEY TEAM

Canada dominated hockey in the early Winter Olympics. In the 1924 Winter Olympics at Chamonix, Canada won all five of its games and outscored the opposition 110–3. The Canadians defeated Czechoslovakia 30–0, Sweden 22–0, Switzerland 33–0, Great Britain 19–2, and the United States 6–1.

4. EMIL ZÁTOPEK

No runner had ever won the 5,000-meter, 10,000-meter, and marathon races at an Olympics until Emil Zátopek of Czechoslovakia won all three in 1952. Zátopek had never run in a marathon prior to his victory in Helsinki.

5. VITALY SCHERBO

At the 1992 Barcelona Olympics, gymnast Vitaly Scherbo of Bélarus won a record six gold medals. Four of them came in a single day when Scherbo won gold medals on four different apparati on August 2.

6. PAAVO NURMI

Paavo Nurmi won the gold medal in the 1,500-meter race at the 1924 Paris Olympics. Less than an hour later, the Flying Finn won the 5,000-meter race.

7. NATALYA LISOVSKAYA

Two-hundred-and-twenty-pound Russian Natalya Lisovskaya easily won the women's shot put competition at the 1998 Seoul Olympics. All six of her throws would have won the gold medal.

8. **PARRY O'BRIEN**

American Parry O'Brien won the gold medal in the shot put at the 1952 Helsinki Olympics. Four years later, at Melbourne, he repeated as the Olympic champion. Any of O'Brien's best five throws would have been good enough to win the competition.

9. **ADEMAR DA SILVA**

Ademar da Silva of Brazil not only won the gold medal in the triple jump at the 1952 Olympics, he broke his own world record four times. Da Silva broke his Olympic record in winning a second gold medal at Melbourne in 1956.

10. **SUZANNE LENGLEN**

Suzanne Lenglen of France defeated Dorothy Holman of Great Britain 6–3, 6–0 to win the gold medal in women's tennis at the 1920 Antwerp Summer Olympics. Lenglen had lost only one game in her previous four matches. From 1919 to 1926, Lenglen lost only one match.

Olympic Royalty

At the 1912 Stockholm Olympics, King Gustav V of Sweden presented decathlon champion Jim Thorpe with the gold medal. The king said, "Sir, you are the greatest athlete in the world." Thorpe replied, "Thanks, king." Since the beginning of the modern Olympics, members of royalty have participated as competitors and officials.

1. BARON DE COUBERTIN

The man most responsible for the revival of the modern Olympic Games was a French nobleman, Pierre de Fredi, better known as Baron de Coubertin. The Olympics resumed in 1896, primarily through the tireless efforts of Coubertin. In 1894, he organized a banquet with athletes from 11 nations performing in events such as mock battles and horse races. Two years later, athletes from 14 nations competed in the first modern Olympics in Athens. King George I of Greece was so pleased with the Olympics that he suggested that they permanently be staged in Athens. Coubertin pretended not to hear him. Instead, the 1900 Olympics were held in Paris.

2. CROWN PRINCE OLAV

At the 1928 Amsterdam Olympics, Crown Prince Olav of Norway won a gold medal as a member of the six-meter yachting crew. In 1957, Olav became King of Norway, and he reigned for 34 years.

3. CROWN PRINCE CONSTANTIN

In 1960, Crown Prince Constantin of Greece won a gold medal as a member of the dragon class sailing crew at the Rome Olympics. To celebrate the victory, the future king was pushed into the water by his mother, Queen Frederika.

4. COUNT HERMANN DE POURTALÈS

The first member of royalty to become an Olympic champion was Count Hermann de Pourtalès of Switzerland. The 53-year-old count was a member of the victorious crew in the one-to-two-ton yachting class at the 1900 Paris Olympics.

5. DUKE KAHANAMOKU

Duke Kahanamoku was a member of Hawaiian royalty. He was named after a family friend, the Duke of Edinburgh. Kahanamoku won gold medals in the 100-meter freestyle swimming competition at the 1912 and 1920 Olympics.

6. NERO

The low point of the ancient Olympics occurred in A.D. 67 when the mad Roman emperor Nero participated in the games. Five thousand spectators were brought to Greece just to cheer the emperor's efforts. While competing in the ten-horse chariot race, Nero was involved in a spill. The officials, fearful of Nero's wrath, helped him back into the chariot and declared him the winner of every event he entered.

7. PRINCE GEORGE OF GREECE

Prince George of Greece was not only a spectator at the 1896 and 1906 Athens Olympics, he served as a judge in several events. In 1896, he was a judge in some of the weightlifting events. In the gymnastic competition, the prince was a judge in the rings event. George was asked to cast the tie-breaking vote when the judges split on whether Ioannis Mitropoulos of Greece or German Hermann Weingärtner should be champion. Not surprisingly, Prince George voted for his countryman. At the 1906 Athens Olympics, Prince George disqualified several competitors in the walking events for improper technique. Questioned for his dubious judging credentials, the prince accepted the criticism in good humor.

8. CHRISTINE VON SALTZA

Sixteen-year-old swimmer Christine Von Saltza won three gold medals at the 1960 Rome Olympics. She won gold in the 400-meter freestyle and as a member of the American 4×100-meter freestyle and 4×100-meter medley teams. Von Saltza's grandfather had been a Swedish count.

9. THE DUCHESS OF WESTMINSTER

The Duchess of Westminster owned a yacht, *Sorais,* that competed in the 1908 Olympics in the eight-meter sailing class. Her crew earned a bronze medal. Apparently, the Duchess not only owned the winning boat but may have been a member of the crew as well.

10. **DARIA PRATT**

Daria Pratt finished third in the women's golf competition at the 1900 Paris Olympics. Years later, the American married Prince Karageorgevich of Serbia.

All in the Family

Pat McCormick won gold medals in both the springboard and platform diving competitions at the 1952 and 1956 Olympics. Her daughter, Kelly, won a silver medal in the springboard at the 1984 Los Angeles Games. Fifty-six-year-old Hilary Smart of the United States won a gold medal in the star class yachting competition at the 1948 Olympics. The other member of the two-man crew was his 23-year-old son, Paul.

The Sundelin brothers, Jörgen, Peter, and Ulf, won a gold medal for Sweden as the crew in the 5.5-meter yachting competition. Twins Bernd and Jörg Landvoigt of the German Democratic Republic won the gold medal in the pair-oared shell without coxswain competition at the 1980 Moscow Olympics. The silver medalists were also twins, Russian brothers Yuri and Nikolai Pimenov.

Andre Agassi won the gold medal in tennis at the 1996 Olympics. His father, Emmanuel, was a boxer on the Iranian team at the 1948 and 1952 Olympics. The gold-medal-winning 1960 United States hockey team had two sets of brothers: Bob and Bill Cleary and Bill and Roger Christian.

1. **PHIL AND STEVE MAHRE**

American Phil Mahre won the gold medal in the slalom competition at the 1984 Sarajevo Winter Olympics. His brother, Steve, finished .21 seconds behind him to capture the silver medal.

2. **NEDO AND ALDO NADI**

Italian Nedo Nadi won five gold medals in fencing events at the 1920 Antwerp Olympics. His brother, Aldo, also won three gold medals in fencing.

3. **LEON AND MICHAEL SPINKS**

Middleweight boxer Michael Spinks won a gold medal at the 1976 Montreal Olympics. His older brother, Leon, won the gold medal in the light heavyweight division. On February 15, 1978, Leon Spinks upset Muhammad Ali to win the heavyweight championship. Seven years later, Michael Spinks won a decision against undefeated Larry Holmes to win the heavyweight title.

4. **VENUS AND SERENA WILLIAMS**

Venus Williams won the gold medal in women's tennis at the 2000 Sydney Olympics. She won a second gold medal when she teamed with sister Serena to win the women's doubles.

5. **HUGH AND REGINALD DOHERTY**

Brothers Hugh and Reginald Doherty of Great Britain were scheduled to play against each other in the semifinals of the tennis competition at the 1900 Olympics. Reginald forfeited the match so that his brother would be rested for the final match against Harold Mahoney of Ireland. Doherty defeated Mahoney 6–4, 6–2, and 6–3. He also teamed with brother Reginald to win the doubles competition.

6. DAVID AND MARK SCHULTZ

Brothers David and Mark Schultz won gold medals in freestyle wrestling at the 1984 Los Angeles Olympics. David won the welterweight division, while Mark was the middle-weight champion.

7. IMRE AND MIKLOS NÉMETH

Imre Németh of Hungary won the gold medal in the hammer throw at the 1948 London Olympics. Miklos, his son, was the gold medalist in the javelin competition at the 1976 Montreal Games.

8. BILL AND FRANK HAVENS

Bill Havens was scheduled to participate in the 1924 Paris Olympics as a member of the American crew in the eight-oared-shell-with-coxswain rowing competition. Havens decided not to compete because his wife was expecting the birth of their first child. As expected, the Americans won the race, and Havens missed his opportunity for a gold medal. In 1952, Frank Havens, the son born during the 1924 Olympics, won a gold medal in the 10,000-meter canoeing singles at the Helsinki Games.

9. HAYES AND DAVID JENKINS

American Hayes Jenkins won the gold medal in figure skating at the 1956 Cortina Olympics. His brother, David, won the bronze medal. Four years later, David won the gold at the 1960 Squaw Valley Games.

10. **WILLIAM AND CHARLOTTE DOD**

William Dod won the men's archery competition at the 1908 London Olympics. Sister Charlotte was the silver medalist in the women's archery competition at the same Games.

Love Games

Over the years, a number of Olympic athletes found romance with other athletes. Bill Toomey, the 1968 decathlon champion, married Mary Rand, the British 1964 long jump medalist. Valery Borzov, the 100-meter-dash gold medalist, married gold medalist gymnast Lyudmila Turischeva.

1. DIANA YORGOVA AND NIKOLAI PRODANOV

Bulgarian long jumper Diana Yorgova and gymnast Nikolai Prodanov were married during the 1964 Tokyo Olympics. They were wed in a Shinto-inspired ceremony at the Olympic village. They had a brief honeymoon in Kyoto. The newlyweds did not medal at the Tokyo Olympics, but Yorgova did win a silver medal at the 1972 Munich Games.

2. VERA CÁSLAVSKÁ AND JOSEF ODLOŽIL

Czech gymnast Vera Cáslavská won four gold medals at the 1968 Mexico City Olympics. That same year, the two-time all-around champion married Josef Odložil, the silver medalist in the 1,500-meter run at the 1964 Olympics. The romance had a tragic ending when Odložil was killed by the couple's teenage son during a dispute in 1993.

3. HAROLD CONNOLLY AND OLGA FIKOTOVÁ

American Harold Connolly won the gold medal in the hammer throw at the 1956 Olympics. In the women's discus, Olga Fikotová of Czechoslovakia won the gold medal. Even though it was the height of the Cold War, Connolly and Fikotová fell in love. They were married in Prague and then moved to the United States. They were divorced in 1973.

4. HELEN STEPHENS AND ADOLF HITLER

Helen Stephens outran Stella Walsh to win the gold medal in the 100-meter sprint at the 1936 Berlin Olympics. While Nazi dictator Adolf Hitler ignored most American medalists, he was absolutely smitten with the six-foot-tall Stephens. The Führer invited her to his private box. According to Stephens, Hitler pinched her rear and suggested that she join him at Berchtesgaden. She politely turned down the Führer's invitation.

5. EMIL ZÁTOPEK AND DANA ZÁTOPKOVA

After winning the 5,000-meter run at the 1952 Helsinki Olympics, Emil Zátopek showed his gold medal to his wife, Dana, prior to her competing in the women's javelin competition. She asked if she could hold on to the medal for good luck. Inspired, she threw the javelin 20 feet farther than her previous best and won her own gold medal.

6. KORNELIA ENDER AND ROLAND MATTHES

Swimmer Kornelia Ender won four gold medals at the 1976 Montreal Olympics. Fellow East German Roland Matthes dominated the backstroke events at the 1968 and 1972 Olympics, also winning four gold medals. Ender and Matthes married in 1978 and divorced four years later.

7. IRINA RODNINA AND ALEKSEI ULANOV

The pairs figure skating competition at the 1972 Sapporo Winter Olympics took on the aspect of a soap opera. Aleksei Ulanov, the partner of Irina Rodnina, became romantically involved with Lyudmila Smirnova, half of the rival Soviet team, Smirnova and Suraikin. Despite the turmoil, Rodnina and Ulanov skated to the gold medal, while Smirnova and Suraikin settled for the silver. After the performance, Rodnina left the ice in tears. Rodnina got a new partner, Aleksandr Zaitsev, and the pair won gold medals in 1976 and 1980.

8. HAYES JENKINS AND CAROL HEISS

Hayes Jenkins won the gold medal in men's figure skating at the 1956 Cortina Olympics. Four years later, another American, Carol Heiss, won the women's figure skating competition. Following their amateur careers, Jenkins and Heiss married.

9. YURI SEDYKH AND LYUDMILA KONDRATYEVA

Yuri Sedykh of the Soviet Union won the hammer throw at the 1976 and 1980 Olympics. Sedykh was married to two Olympic champions, 1980 100-meter-dash gold medalist Lyudmila Kondratyeva and 1988 shot-put winner Natalaya Lisovskaya.

10. NADIA COMANECI AND BART CONNER

Romanian gymnast Nadia Comaneci won the women's all-around competition at the 1976 Olympics. American Bart Conner won a gold medal in the parallel bars at the 1984 Los Angeles Games. Comaneci and Conner were married in 1996.

Fourteen-year-old gymnast Nadia Comaneci scored seven perfect tens at the 1976 Montreal Olympics.

Women Athletes

The modern Olympics have been in existence for more than a century, and women athletes are now just beginning to gain equality. In the beginning, the modern Olympics were predominantly athletic contests for men. It was thought that sports were too strenuous for women or unladylike. Some believed that women engaging in competitive sports would become sterile or age prematurely.

1. KALLIPATERIA

In the ancient Olympics, women were barred from competing. Married women faced a penalty of death if they were ever found watching an event. Kallipateria was the mother of an Olympic boxer named Pisirodos. She risked death by disguising herself as his trainer. When Pisirodos won the competition, his mother, in her excitement, jumped over the trainers' barrier, exposing herself. The officials spared her life because her father, brother, and son had all been Olympic champions. To make sure that it never happened again, they passed a law that all trainers had to be naked.

2. THE 1896 ATHENS OLYMPICS

All 295 athletes at the 1896 Athens Olympics were male. At the 1900 Paris Games, only 11 of 1,077 competitors were female. Four years later, only 6 women athletes competed at the St. Louis Olympics.

3. MELPOMENE

A Greek woman named Melpomene petitioned to participate in the 1896 marathon. When officials refused to let a woman compete, Melpomene decided to run the race on her own. She started minutes after the men runners had begun. Taunted by spectators, she stopped for ten minutes at Pikermi to rest and drink water. Replenished, she passed many of the male contestants. Not permitted to enter the stadium, she ran her final lap around the arena.

4. THE 1928 800-METER RACE

Women's track events did not become Olympic events until the 1928 Amsterdam Games. Races were scheduled for 100 and 800 meters. The longer race turned out to be a disaster that set back women's Olympic track for decades. Lina Radke of Germany won the 800 meters; however, several of the other competitors collapsed from exhaustion.

The president of the International Olympic Committee, Comte de Baillet-Latour, proposed that women's sports be eliminated from the Olympics. The proposal was ignored, but the 800-meter race for women was not run again until the 1960 Rome Olympics.

5. THERESA WELD

American figure skater Theresa Weld won the bronze medal at the 1920 Antwerp Olympics. Her athleticism was actually a liability. One judge cautioned her against attempting jumps he deemed "unsuitable for a lady."

6. FANNY DURACK

Women's swimming did not become an Olympic event until the 1912 Stockholm Games. The winner of the 100-meter freestyle was Australian Sarah "Fanny" Durack. Since the Australian Olympic Committee considered it a waste of money to send women to the Olympics, Durack's family had to raise money to pay her way.

7. JOAN BENOIT

The belief that women were unable to compete in long-distance running events was shattered at the 1984 Los Angeles Olympics when the first women's marathon was run. Winner Joan Benoit won the race in a time of 2:24:52. She felt so strong at the finish that she said she could have turned around and run another 26 miles.

8. STACY DRAGILA

The women's pole vault did not become an Olympic event until the 2000 Sydney Games. The first gold medalist was American Stacy Dragila.

9. **SHABANA AKHTAR**

Pakistan's Shabana Akhtar finished thirty-fourth in the long jump at the 1996 Atlanta Olympics. Although Pakistan had been sending athletes to the Olympics since 1948, Akhtar was the first woman to represent that country.

10. **WOMEN'S BASKETBALL**

Men's basketball became an Olympic event in 1936. Women's basketball did not become an Olympic event until 1976. The team from the Soviet Union won the first gold medal in women's basketball.

African-American Athletes

B lack athletes such as Jesse Owens and Carl Lewis have starred at the Olympics. The African-American athletes in this list helped eliminate racial barriers in their Olympic sports.

1. GEORGE POAGE

George Poage was the first African-American athlete to win a medal in a track event. At the 1904 St. Louis Olympics, Poage won bronze medals in the 200- and 400-meter hurdle races.

2. JOSEPH STADLER

The first African-American to win a silver medal was Joseph Stadler. He finished second in the standing high jump at the 1904 Olympics.

3. JOHN TAYLOR

In 1908, John Taylor became the first African-American to win a gold medal. He won as a member of the American 4 × 400-meter relay team. Sadly, Taylor died of typhoid fever four months later.

The star of the 1936 Berlin Olympics, Jesse Owens won multiple gold medals while breaking down racial barriers.

4. HOWARD DREW

The United States has been represented by many great black sprinters in Olympic competition. Jesse Owens, Bob Hayes, and Carl Lewis were all 100-meter-dash champions. The first great black sprinter was Howard Drew. At the 1912 Olympic trials, Drew defeated Ralph Craig, the eventual Olympic champion in the 100-meter dash. Drew won his qualifying heat at the 1912 Stockholm Olympics but injured his tendon and was unable to compete in the finals.

5. WILLIAM DEHART HUBBARD

The first African-American to win a gold medal in an individual event was William Dehart Hubbard. He jumped 24 feet, 5 inches, to win the long jump at the 1924 Paris Olympics.

6. AUDREY PATTERSON

Audrey Patterson was the first African-American woman to win an Olympic medal. Patterson won a bronze medal in the 200-meter dash at the 1948 London Games.

7. ALICE COACHMAN

On August 7, 1948, Alice Coachman became the first African-American woman to win a gold medal at the Games. She placed first in the high jump at the 1948 London Olympics.

8. DON BARKSDALE

The first black basketball player to be a member of the United States Olympic team was Don Barksdale. He played on the gold-medal-winning 1948 team.

9. DEBI THOMAS

Debi Thomas made history in 1988 when she became the first black figure skater to medal in the women's competition. Thomas won the bronze medal as German Katarina Witt secured her second consecutive Olympic title.

10. WILLIE DAVENPORT

Willie Davenport won a gold medal in the 110-meter hurdles at the 1968 Mexico City Summer Olympics. Twelve years later, at Lake Placid, Davenport became the first African-American to participate in the Winter Olympics. Davenport competed in the bobsled event but did not medal.

Discontinued Events

There have been some strange events held at the Olympics. One of the oddest was the dueling pistols competition at the 1906 Athens Games. Competitors shot at mannequins dressed in frock coats. A bull's eye was painted on the dummy's throat. Leon Moreaux of France won the gold medal.

1. ANTHROPOLOGY DAYS

The 1904 St. Louis Olympics staged one of the most unusual and shameful events in the Games' history. Anthropology Days featured athletic competitions between so-called primitive peoples from around the world.

The athletes included Pygmies, Patagonians, Filipinos (Moros), Native Americans (Sioux), Mexicans (Cocopa), and Japanese (Ainus). The competitions included mud fighting and a greased-pole climb, as well as track and field events.

Organizers said that the idea was to see if "savages" could compete in athletic contests. When he heard about Anthropology Days, Baron de Coubertin was appalled. "As for that outrageous charade, it will, of course, lose its appeal when black men, red men, and yellow men learn to run, jump, and throw and leave the white men behind them."

2. THE 100-METER FREESTYLE FOR SAILORS

An unusual event at the 1896 Athens Olympics was a 100-meter freestyle swimming race for sailors. The competition was limited to sailors in the Greek navy. The winner of the event was Ioannis Malokinis.

3. LIVE PIGEON SHOOTING

Live pigeon shooting was an event at the 1900 Paris Olympics. The object of the competition was to shoot and kill as many pigeons as possible. A contestant was eliminated when he missed two birds. Nearly 300 pigeons were dispatched in this manner. An award of 20,000 francs was to be awarded to the winner. However, the top four finishers agreed to split the prize money equally.

4. ALL-AROUND DUMBBELL CONTEST

In 1904, there was an event known as the all-around dumbbell contest at the St. Louis Olympics. The weightlifting competition consisted of nine different kinds of lifts. Oscar Osthoff of the United States won.

5. 200-METER OBSTACLE RACE

The 200-meter obstacle race at the 1900 Paris Olympics was a combination of a swimming race and obstacle course. Swimmers were required to climb over a pole and then climb over and swim under a row of boats. Frederick Lane of Australia was the first and only champion in the obstacle run.

6. UNDERWATER SWIMMING

Another oddity of the Paris Olympics was an underwater swimming competition. Swimmers were awarded two points for each meter swam underwater and one point for each second they were able to remain submerged. The winner was Charles de Vendeville of France. Third-place finisher Peder Lykkeberg of Denmark actually remained underwater for 22 seconds more than Vendeville but lost because he swam in a circle.

7. THE PLUNGE FOR DISTANCE

The plunge for distance was an Olympic event at the 1904 St. Louis Games. The idea was to dive into the water and swim as far as possible without taking a breath in one minute. The contestant who had traveled the farthest in the pool was the winner. American William Dickey won with a distance of 62 feet, 6 inches.

8. ROPE CLIMBING

Believe it or not, rope climbing was an Olympic event from 1896 to 1932. At the first Olympics, only two competitors reached the top of the 14-meter-high rope. Nikolaus Andriakopoulos of Greece was the first winner.

9. CROQUET

Croquet was the least-popular event in the annals of the Olympics. Only one spectator, an Englishman, paid to watch the croquet matches at the 1900 Paris Olympics. The French swept the medals in both the men's and women's competitions.

10. **PUTTING CONTEST**

A putting contest was held at the 1904 St. Louis Olympics. The competition took place at the Glen Echo Golf Club. Fifty-two-year-old American Burt McKinnie won, even though he needed 21 putts for the nine holes.

Weird Venues

The wrestling matches at the 1896 Athens Games were contested in a sand pit. Here are some of the most unlikely locations for Olympic events.

1. 1900 PARIS TRACK AND FIELD

The track and field facilities for the 1900 Paris Olympics left something to be desired. There was no cinder track, only a 500-meter oval in the grass. No pits were provided for the pole vaulters, who had to jam their poles into the ground. During the competition, animal exhibits were housed nearby; the stench was sometimes overwhelming.

2. 1900 PARIS DISCUS COMPETITION

One of the athletes to suffer from the bizarre conditions at the 1900 Paris Olympics was 1896 discus champion Robert Garrett. The narrow field where the discus event was held was lined by trees. Garrett's best throws hit limbs of the trees, and he did not medal. Hungarian Rudolf Bauer's throws had less arc, and he won the gold medal.

3. **1900 PARIS 400-METER HURDLES**

The 400-meter hurdles competition at the Paris Olympics was the strangest on record. The hurdles were telephone poles, and a water jump was placed near the finish line. American John Tewksbury won the event with a time of 57.6 seconds.

4. **1992 BARCELONA SAILING COMPETITIONS**

The sailing competitions at the 1992 Olympics were held in the Parc de Mar, located in Barcelona harbor. The water was so polluted that garbage and dead rats floated on the surface. In the sailboard competition, the mess cost American Michael Gebhardt the gold medal when a bag of garbage caught on his boat. By the time Gebhardt pulled it off, he had been passed by several competitors. He settled for the silver medal as Franck David of France won the gold.

5. **1904 ST. LOUIS MARATHON**

The marathon course for the 1904 St. Louis Olympics can best be described as a nightmare. Most of the race was run on dusty roads. Automobiles transporting journalists and officials kicked up clouds of dust. One runner, Bill Garcia, suffered a stomach hemorrhage because he inhaled so much dust. Runners constantly dodged the automobiles, and two officials were injured when their car crashed after swerving to avoid a runner. An African runner, Jan Mashiani, was chased off the course and through a cornfield by two dogs.

6. **1920 ANTWERP SWIMMING COMPETITIONS**

Today, Olympic swimming events are held in state-of-the-art pools. At the 1920 Antwerp Olympics, swimming competitions were held in a ditch filled with freezing water. Several of the female swimmers were carried from the water nearly unconscious.

7. 1920 ANTWERP CYCLING

The cycling venue at the 1920 Antwerp Olympics was no better than the swimming facilities. Cyclists had to navigate through the streets of the city. The course crossed a train track, and cyclists often had to wait for a passing train. Officials stationed at the crossing kept track of the time lost waiting for trains. In the road time trial, Henry Kaltenbrun of South Africa was about to be declared the winner when it was learned that Harry Stengvist of Sweden had been delayed four minutes by a passing train.

8. 2000 SYDNEY GYMNASTIC COMPETITION

The women's vaulting competition at the 2000 Sydney Olympics was disrupted by an improperly installed horse. The height of the horse from which the gymnasts vaulted was set at 120 centimeters instead of the standard 125 centimeters. As a result, many competitors were thrown off by the two-inch mistake. American Elise Ray nearly missed the horse entirely and landed on her back. The biggest victim was Sveltlana Khorkina of Russia, one of the favorites to win the all-around competition. Khorkina landed on her knees during the vault and was so shaken that she also fell on the uneven bars. When it was discovered that the horse was incorrectly set, the gymnasts were offered a chance to redo their vault. Khorkina, whose dream of a gold medal was shattered by her poor uneven bars performance, declined to attempt a second vault. Although she did not medal in the all-around, she did win a gold medal in the uneven bars competition.

9. 1956 STOCKHOLM EQUESTRIAN EVENTS

The 1956 Summer Olympics were held in Melbourne, Australia. Because of a six-month quarantine on horses entering the country, the equestrian events were staged around the world in Stockholm, Sweden.

10. 1896 ATHENS TRACK EVENTS

The track at the 1896 Athens Olympics had such sharp turns that runners actually had to slow down to keep from falling. As a result, the times for the running events were exceptionally slow.

Not Fit for Man nor Beast

M any Olympic events are held outdoors and are at the mercy of weather conditions. During the clay trap shooting at the 1908 London Olympics, heavy rains and high winds delayed the beginning of the competition. By the time the event started, it was so late that the targets were painted white so the shooters could see them in the dark sky.

1. 1896 ATHENS ROWING COMPETITIONS

The rowing competitions at the 1896 Athens Olympics were scheduled as the last events. All seven races were supposed to be run on the same day. High winds and a cold rain made conditions unsuitable for competition. Boats were swept ashore by the rough seas. Officials were forced to cancel all the rowing events.

2. 1900 PARIS MARATHON

The 1900 marathon at the Paris Olympics was run in the midst of a heat wave. The 102-degree temperature caused runners to drop out at such a pace that only seven competitors finished. The only one to break three hours was Michel Théato of Luxembourg.

3. 1904 ST. LOUIS MARATHON

The weather at the 1904 St. Louis marathon was barely more tolerable than in Paris. Runners struggled in the 90-degree heat. American William Garcia, one of the early leaders, was found unconscious on the side of the road, suffering from dehydration and heat exhaustion. Another American, Jack Lordon, withdrew after ten miles following a vomiting attack. Thomas Hicks won the race in a time of 3:28:53, nearly a half an hour slower than the winning time in Paris four years earlier.

4. 1896 ATHENS 100-METER FREESTYLE

The 100-meter freestyle swimming race at the Athens Olympics was held in the Bay of Zea on April 11, 1896. The water temperature was a frigid 53 degrees. An American swimmer, Gardner Williams, reportedly jumped out of the water, exclaiming, "It's freezing." The race was run between two buoys. The lane markers were hollow pumpkins that floated with the tide, making the course difficult to follow. The winner, Alfred Hajos of Hungary, covered himself with a half-inch layer of grease as protection against the cold.

5. 1936 MUNICH BASKETBALL FINALS

The 1936 gold-medal men's basketball game between the United States and Canada was played outdoors on a court made of clay and sand. The surface was turned to mud by heavy rains. Players had difficulty gripping and dribbling the wet basketball. The United States prevailed by the score of 19–8.

6. **1928 ST. MORITZ 10,000-METER SPEED SKATING**

The 10,000-meter speed-skating competition at St. Moritz, Switzerland, in 1928 was marred by rising temperatures. After the first heat, American Irving Jaffee was the leader. The ice began to melt as the temperature rose, and officials were forced to halt the event. They hoped to rerun the race, but the competitors, recognizing Jaffee as the winner, refused. Four years later at Lake Placid, Jaffee repeated as Olympic champion in the 10,000 meters.

7. **1928 ST. MORITZ 50-KILOMETER NORDIC SKIING**

The 50-kilometer cross-country ski race at the St. Moritz Games was held on February 14, 1928, the same day as the 10,000-meter speed-skating race. Temperatures, which began close to zero, rose to the high 70s by the time the race was completed. Per Erik Hedlund of Sweden overcame the unusual weather to finish more than 13 minutes ahead of his closest rival.

8. **1988 SEOUL 470 SAILING CLASS**

The 470 sailing class competition at the 1988 Seoul Olympics was held in nearly gale-force winds. In one of the heats, the boat of Joseph Chan of the Singapore team capsized. Chan was rescued by another competitor, Lawrence Lemieux of Canada. Lemieux, who was in second place at the time, eventually finished twenty-second. Lemieux was commended for his heroism but did not medal in the event.

9. **1932 50-KILOMETER NORDIC SKIING**

The 50-kilometer cross-country ski race at the 1932 Lake Placid Olympics was held in near-blizzard conditions. The gold medalist was Veli Saarinen of Finland.

10. 1972 MUNICH SOCCER FINALS

The soccer gold-medal game between Poland and Hungary at the 1972 Munich Olympics was contested in a rainstorm. High winds made play difficult. Poland won the game 2–1. All three goals were scored with the wind behind the scorer's back.

You Can Look It Up

At the 1896 Athens Olympics, the German gymnastic association threatened its athletes with suspension if they competed. Despite the warning, gymnasts Carl Schuhmann, Hermann Weingärtner, and Alfred Flatow became Olympic champions.

All 14 men on the American Olympic team at the 1896 Games were members of the Boston Athletic Association. Their expenses were paid through the fundraising efforts of a Massachusetts politician named Oliver Ames. Ellery Clark, the first Olympic high-jump champion, was permitted to compete only if he promised not to mention that he was a student at Harvard University.

Figure skating was an event in the Summer Olympics from 1908 to 1920. Here are some more Olympic believe-it-or-nots.

1. 1928 ST. MORITZ FOUR-MAN BOBSLED TEAM

Three members of the gold-medal-winning American four-man bobsled team at the 1928 St. Moritz Olympics had never been in a bobsled until less than a month before the

Games began. Nion Tucker, Geoffrey Mason, and Richard Parke were selected by answering an ad placed in the Paris edition of the *New York Tribune.* They began practice only 18 days prior to the race. The driver of the sled was 16-year-old Billy Fiske.

2. **MARGARET ABBOTT**

In 1900, American Margaret Abbott won the women's golf competition at the Paris Olympics. She was studying art in Paris at the time and was totally unaware that she was competing in the Olympics. Abbott believed she had entered a local golf tournament. She received an Old Saxon porcelain bowl in chiseled gold for her victory. When she died in 1955, Abbott was still unaware that she was an Olympic champion.

3. **HENRY PEARCE**

Australian Henry Pearce won the gold medal in the single sculls rowing competition at the 1928 Amsterdam Olympics. He was so superior to his competition that he actually stopped to let a line of ducks pass in front of his boat and still won the race easily.

4. **GIOVANNI PETTENELLA**

Strategy plays a big part in sprint cycling. Cyclists will slow to a stop to try to get an opponent to make the first move. At the 1964 Tokyo Olympics, Giovanni Pettenella of Italy and Pierre Trentin of France were matched against each other in the 1,000-meter sprint semifinals. They stood still for a record 21 minutes and 57 seconds. Pettenella won the race and went on to win the gold medal.

5. **ANDREA MEAD LAWRENCE**

In the first run of the women's slalom at the 1952 Oslo Olympics, American Andrea Mead Lawrence caught her ski on a gate and lost her balance. Most skiers quit after missing a gate, but Lawrence quickly regained her balance, backtracked to complete the gate, and finished her run in fourth place. Lawrence had an incredible second run and shocked everyone by winning the gold medal.

6. **MAGDA JULIN**

Magda Julin of Sweden won the gold medal in women's figure skating at the 1920 Antwerp Olympics despite receiving no first-place ordinals from the judges. Svea Noren of Sweden, Theresa Weld of the United States, Phyllis Johnson of Great Britain, and Margot Mot of Norway all received first-place votes, but Julin won on the strength of having three second-place ordinals.

7. **BEATRIX LOUGHRAN**

American Beatrix Loughran won the bronze medal in women's figure skating at the 1928 St. Moritz Olympics. The panel of judges had widely differing opinions on the quality of her skating. One judge actually placed Loughran first, ahead of gold medalist Sonja Henie. The other judges placed her second, third, fourth, fifth, sixth, and seventh.

8. **ERIK VILÉN**

Despite finishing third in the 400-meter hurdles at the 1924 Paris Olympics, Erik Vilén of Finland was credited with an Olympic record. First-place finisher Morgan Taylor of the

United States was not credited with an Olympic record because he knocked down a hurdle. At the time, an athlete who knocked down a hurdle was ineligible to set an Olympic record. Second-place finisher Charles Brookins of the United States was disqualified for improperly clearing a hurdle. Vilén, despite crossing the finish line third, was awarded the silver medal and credited with an Olympic record.

9. DORA RATJEN

German Dora Ratjen finished fourth in the women's high jump at the 1936 Berlin Olympics. Two years later, Ratjen was banned from international competition when it was discovered that the athlete was a hermaphrodite. In 1957, Ratjen claimed he had been ordered to pose as a woman by the Nazi Youth Movement.

10. 1948 UNITED STATES HOCKEY TEAM

Due to a dispute over which organization was the governing body of amateur hockey in America, the United States sent two hockey teams to the 1948 St. Moritz Olympics. One team was backed by the American Hockey Association and the other by the Amateur Athletic Association. The St. Moritz Olympic officials recognized the AHA team, which won five of its eight games, including a 31–1 blowout of Italy, but did not medal. At some of the games, players from the other American team sat in the stands and booed their compatriots.

Overcoming Handicaps

Tamás Darnyi of Hungary won gold medals in the 200-meter individual medley at the 1988 and 1992 Olympics despite being blind in his left eye. He is one of many athletes who have overcome severe physical handicaps to compete in the Olympics.

1. GEORGE EYSER

American George Eyser lost his left leg when he was run over by a train as a youth. Despite competing with a wooden leg, Eyser won gold medals in the parallel bar and long horse of the 1904 St. Louis Olympics. The gymnast also earned medals in the side horse, horizontal bar, and combined exercise events. Eyser won a third gold medal in the rope-climbing competition.

2. KÁROLY TAKÁCS

The shooting career of Hungarian Károly Takács appeared to be over in 1938 when a defective grenade exploded in his right hand during a military exercise. He taught himself to shoot with his left hand and won gold medals in the rapid-fire pistol competitions at the 1948 and 1952 Olympics.

3. **JIM ABBOTT**

Born without a right hand, Jim Abbott overcame his handicap to become an outstanding baseball pitcher. Baseball was a demonstration event at the 1988 Seoul Olympics. Abbott pitched the United States to a 5–3 victory over Japan in the championship game. Abbott had an outstanding career as a major-league pitcher, highlighted by a no-hitter for the New York Yankees on September 4, 1993.

4. **OLIVÉR HALASSY**

Olivér Halassy was a member of the gold-medal Hungarian water-polo teams in 1932 and 1936. Halassy was an outstanding player despite having had one of his legs amputated below the knee. The injury was the result of a streetcar accident when he was a youth.

5. **PAOLA FANTATO**

Italian Paola Fantato competed in the archery competition at the 1996 Atlanta Olympics while seated in a wheelchair. Fantato had been paralyzed by polio. Although Fantato did not medal, the archer was an inspiration for other physically challenged athletes.

6. **MARLA RUNYAN**

Marla Runyan qualified for the women's 1,500-meter run at the 2000 Sydney Games with a third-place finish in the United States Olympic trials. Runyan's accomplishment was miraculous considering that she suffers from Stargardt's disease, a degenerative retina condition that limits her vision. Able to see only peripherally, Runyan sees other runners as streaks of light. Runyan finished eighth in the women's 1,500 meters at Sydney.

7. PYAMBUU TUUL

Mongolian marathoner Pyambuu Tuul was blinded by an explosion in 1978. Despite being unable to see, Tuul competed in marathons with the help of a guide. A year before the 1992 Olympics, an operation restored partial sight to his right eye. Although he finished far behind the winner, Tuul did complete the marathon at the 1992 Barcelona Olympics.

8. ILDIKÓ UJLAKI-REJTÖ

Born deaf, Hungarian fencer Ildikó Ujlaki-Rejtö won a gold medal in the individual foil at the 1964 Tokyo Olympics. Four years later, she won a bronze medal in the same event at the Mexico City Games.

9. HAROLD CONNOLLY

Harold Connolly began throwing the hammer while at Boston College to strengthen his arm. Connolly had his left arm broken several times while playing football, and it was four inches shorter than his right. Connolly overcame the handicap and won the gold medal in the hammer throw at the 1956 Melbourne Olympics.

10. MURRAY HALBERG

Murray Halberg suffered serious injuries during a rugby match in 1950. His left arm was paralyzed, and he spent two months in the hospital. Despite his withered arm, he became an outstanding athlete. At the 1960 Rome Olympics, the New Zealand runner won the gold medal in the 5,000-meter run.

Wilma Rudolph suffered from numerous childhood illnesses, which left her limping with a leg brace for many of her early years. With the strength and determination of a true Olympian, she overcame her disability to win three gold medals at the 1960 Rome Olympics.

Amazing Recoveries

S helly Mann was stricken by polio at the age of six. She took up swimming to strengthen her legs. In 1956, Mann won the gold medal in the women's 100-meter butterfly at the Melbourne Summer Olympics.

All of these athletes recovered from debilitating illnesses to compete in the Olympics.

1. LIS HARTEL

Lis Hartel was stricken by polio in 1944. Paralyzed below the knees, Hartel overcame the odds and continued competing in equestrian events. The Danish rider, who needed help to mount and dismount her horse, won a silver medal in the individual dressage event in 1952 and 1956.

2. WILMA RUDOLPH

As a child, Rudolph suffered several serious illnesses, including double pneumonia, scarlet fever, and polio. For most of her childhood, Rudolph wore a brace on her left leg. Incredibly, Rudolph won gold medals in the 100- and 200-meter dashes at the 1960 Rome Olympics. She won her third gold medal as a member of the American 4×100-meter relay team.

3. RAY EWRY

Ray Ewry contracted polio as a child and for a time was confined to a wheelchair. He did jumping exercises to strengthen his legs. Eventually he became an incredible jumper. Between 1900 and 1908, Ewry won ten gold medals in standing high-jump events.

4. JEFF BLATNICK

Prior to the 1984 Los Angeles Olympics, no American had ever won a medal in Greco-Roman wrestling. Super heavyweight Jeff Blatnick ended the drought by winning a gold medal at the Los Angeles Games. Only two years before his Olympic victory, Blatnick had been diagnosed with Hodgkin's disease and had his spleen and appendix removed.

5. WALTER DAVIS

Walter Davis was unable to walk for three years as a child due to a bout with polio. Davis not only won a gold medal in the high jump at the 1952 Helsinki Olympics, he had a successful career as a basketball player in the NBA.

6. DICK ROTH

American swimmer Dick Roth was stricken with appendicitis three days before he was scheduled to compete in the 400-meter individual medley at the 1964 Tokyo Olympics. Despite incredible pain, Roth delayed the operation and won the gold medal.

7. GAIL DEVERS

Sprinter Gail Devers suffered from Graves' Disease in the four years prior to the 1992 Barcelona Olympics. Complications from the disease nearly resulted in her having her feet amputated. Devers capped an amazing comeback by winning gold medals in the 100-meter dash at the 1992 and 1996 Olympics.

8. TOIVO LOUKOLA

In the early 1920s, Toivo Loukola contracted tuberculosis. He took up running to regain his health. The Finnish athlete won a gold medal in the 3,000-meter steeplechase at the 1928 Amsterdam Olympics.

9. DEBORAH CAMPAGNOLI

In 1990, Italian skier Deborah Campagnoli underwent emergency surgery in which more than a foot of her intestines was removed. Two years later, she won a gold medal in the Super G event at the 1992 Albertville Winter Olympics.

10. TENLEY ALBRIGHT

Tenley Albright contracted polio at the age of 11. Albright won a gold medal in women's figure skating at the 1956 Cortina Olympics. After her skating career was over, Albright became a doctor.

Incredible Injuries

Two weeks prior to the date he was scheduled to run in the marathon at the 1984 Los Angeles Olympics, Portuguese runner Carlos Lopes was struck by a car. He was thrown through the windshield, but, miraculously, his injuries were not serious. Despite the accident, Lopes went on to win the marathon and set an Olympic record. All of these athletes were injured just prior to or during the Olympics.

1. SHUN FUJIMOTO

During the team combined exercises at the 1976 Montreal Olympics, Japanese gymnast Shun Fujimoto broke his kneecap during the floor exercise competition. Not wishing to disturb his teammates, Fujimoto concealed the severity of his injury. Amazingly, he performed credibly on the side-horse. He completed an excellent routine on the rings, but on the dismount, he dislocated his already injured knee. Forced to miss the rest of the competition, Fujimoto's heroics were rewarded as the Japanese won the gold medal in the team competition.

2. KONRAD VON WANGENHEIM

Germany won the three-day team equestrian competition at the 1936 Berlin Olympics thanks to the courage of Konrad von Wangenheim. He broke his collarbone in a fall during the endurance run. Despite tremendous pain, he remounted and finished the course. The following day, his horse reared and fell back on him. Once again, he ignored the pain and completed the run. His heroics were rewarded with the gold medal.

3. VLADIMIR LAPITSKY

Russian fencer Vladimir Lapitsky was injured in a freak accident during the team foil competition at the 1980 Moscow Olympics. Lapitsky was stabbed in the chest when the foil of his Polish opponent broke. A blood vessel was severed, but he still won a silver medal as the Russians finished second to France.

4. BILL ROYCROFT

Australian Bill Roycroft broke his collarbone in a fall during the endurance phase of the three-day equestrian team event at the 1960 Rome Olympics. Roycroft insisted on finishing the competition and led Australia to the gold medal.

5. JÓHANNES JÓSEFSSON

An injury cost Greco-Roman wrestler Jóhannes Jósefsson a chance at a medal at the 1908 London Olympics. The middleweight from Iceland broke his arm in the semifinal match and was unable to continue.

6. GEORGE CANE

George Cane of Great Britain competed in the men's plain high-diving competition at the 1908 London Olympics. On one of his dives, Cane was knocked unconscious. He nearly drowned before he was pulled from the water by officials. Cane finished the competition but did not medal.

7. MICKI KING

American Micki King led after eight dives in the springboard diving competition at the 1968 Mexico City Olympics. On her ninth dive, she broke her left arm when she struck the diving board. King just missed a medal with a fourth-place finish. Four years later, at the Munich Olympics, King won the gold medal in springboard diving.

8. VASSILIOS PAPAGEORGOPOULOUS

Greek sprinter Vassilios Papageorgopoulous recorded the fastest time in the first heat of the 100-meter dash at the 1972 Munich Olympics. Unfortunately, he injured his groin and was unable to race in the final.

9. MELVIN PENDER

Melvin Pender of the United States was considered a contender for a medal in the 100-meter sprint at the 1964 Tokyo Olympics. Pender tore a rib muscle in one of the heats. Ignoring the advice of doctors, he ran in the final and finished sixth. Pender was hospitalized after the race.

10. KÁROLY VARGA

Two days before he was to compete in the small-bore rifle competition at the 1980 Moscow Olympics, Károly Varga of Hungary broke his shooting hand. Despite the injury, he won the gold medal.

Lucky Stars

These athletes can thank their lucky stars for their Olympic success.

1. PARRY O'BRIEN

Parry O' Brien won the gold medal in the shot put at the 1952 Helsinki Olympics. He passed his lucky sweatshirt to Sim Inness, who won the discus competition the next day. The sweatshirt was then given to Cy Young, who won the gold medal in the javelin. Young tried to pass the sweatshirt to Jack Davis, an American 110-meter hurdles competitor. Davis decided not to wear the sweaty shirt and finished second to Harrison Dillard.

2. LYDIA SKOBLIKOVA

Prior to the 1964 Innsbruck Winter Olympics, the wife of the United States speed-skating coach gave a good-luck pin to a Soviet speed skater, Lydia Skoblikova. Skoblikova won four gold medals at the Innsbruck Games.

3. IVAN BROWN

Ivan Brown teamed with Alan Washbond to form America's leading two-man bobsled at the 1936 Garmisch Winter Olympics. Brown had a superstition that he needed to find a hairpin on the ground each day to be lucky. Incredibly, he found hairpins for 24 consecutive days prior to the Olympic two-man bobsled competition. With these good-luck omens adding to his confidence, Brown won a gold medal.

4. PIERRE D'ORIOLA

Christian d'Oriola won a gold medal in the individual foil-fencing competition at the 1952 Helsinki Olympics. Christian gave his lucky white cap to his cousin, Pierre, who was scheduled to compete in the individual jumping equestrian competition. Pierre d'Oriola duplicated Christian's performance by winning a gold medal.

5. CHRIS VON SALTZA

American swimmer Chris Von Saltza always took her lucky toy frog to competitions. At the 1960 Rome Olympics, she won three gold medals.

6. GEORGE ROTH

George Roth had one of his daughter's baby booties placed inside his shoe for luck during the club-swinging competition at the 1932 Los Angeles Olympics. Roth won the gold medal, but club swinging was discontinued as an Olympic event after the 1932 Games.

7. ANNE HENNING

Speed skater Anne Henning may have set a record for lucky charms. At the 1972 Sapporo Winter Olympics, Henning had a Snoopy doll, four-leaf clover, Christmas ornament, and Japanese beads to give her luck. Henning set an Olympic record and won a gold medal in the 500-meter speed-skating competition.

8. CHARLEY PADDOCK

On his way to the starting line for the 100-meter dash at the 1920 Antwerp Olympics, American Charley Paddock knocked on a piece of wood that he thought brought him luck. Luck or not, Paddock won the gold medal.

9. RANDY WILLIAMS

Randy Williams carried a lucky teddy bear to the long-jump competition at the 1972 Munich Olympics. Williams jumped 27 feet to win the gold medal.

10. WILLIAM PETERSSON

William Petersson of Sweden noticed a coin on the runway before his first turn in the long-jump competition at the 1920 Antwerp Olympics. For good luck, he put the coin in his left shoe. Petersson won the gold medal.

No Luck at All

L ady luck did not smile on these Olympic athletes.

1. JULES NOËL

Frenchman Jules Noël appeared to have the longest throw
of the competition in the discus event at the 1932 Los
Angeles Olympics. But officials, who were distracted by the
pole-vault competition that was going on at the same time,
did not notice where the throw had landed. Noël was given
another throw but could not duplicate his best. The unfortunate Noël finished fourth, just missing a medal.

2. JACOB TULLIN THAMS

Ski jumper Jacob Tullin Thams actually jumped too far for his
own good. The Norwegian had won a gold medal in the 90-
meter ski jump at the 1924 Chamonix Olympics. He was not
so lucky at the 1928 St. Moritz Winter Games. Thams jumped
73 meters—nine meters farther than the next best jump in
the competition. Unfortunately, the hill was not long enough

to accommodate the jump, and he fell on the flat landing surface. Penalized for style points, he finished in twenty-eighth place.

3. KARL SCHRANZ

One of the unluckiest athletes in Winter Olympic history was skier Karl Schranz of Austria. In the slalom competition at the 1968 Grenoble Winter Olympics, Schranz was given a second run when a spectator unexpectedly ran into his path. His second run was good enough to win the gold medal. Hours after the race, however, officials disqualified Schranz for missing a gate prior to encountering the spectator. Schranz hoped to win his gold medal at the 1972 Sapporo Games, but he was banned from the Olympics for having accepted money from sponsors.

4. WERNER GÜNTHÖR

Swiss shot putter Werner Günthör unleashed a throw of 71 feet, 6 inches at the 1992 Barcelona Olympics. The throw would have been good enough for the gold medal, but Günthör lost his balance on the follow-through and touched his fingers to the ground. The foul cost him his chance at a gold medal. Günthör's next-best throw was three feet shorter, and he finished fourth.

5. CHRISTIAN GITSHAM

In the marathon at the 1912 Stockholm Olympics, South African runners Christian Gitsham and Kenneth McArthur were the leaders two miles from the finish. Gitsham wanted to stop for a drink of water, and his friend McArthur told him he would stop and wait for him. Instead, McArthur kept running and went on to finish nearly a minute ahead of Gitsham. At the 1920 Olympics, Gitsham was leading the marathon when his shoe split, and he was forced to drop out.

6. **TERRY MCDERMOTT**

Terry McDermott won the gold medal in the 500-meter speed-skating race at the 1964 Innsbruck Olympics. He was the favorite to repeat as champion at the 1968 Grenoble Olympics. The day of the 500-meter race was warmer than usual, and the ice began to melt. McDermott had the bad luck to draw in the last pair. The melting ice made the times progressively slower as the day went on. Despite the bad draw, McDermott finished second. If he had skated earlier, he would almost certainly have won the gold medal.

7. **JAMES MITCHEL**

The stone throw was an event at the 1906 Athens Olympics. Competitors were required to throw a 14-pound weight. The favorite was expected to be American James Mitchel. However, on the voyage to Athens, Mitchel injured his shoulder in a fall when the ship was tossed during rough seas. Mitchel was unable to compete. His bad luck continued when the stone throw was discontinued as an Olympic event.

8. **DAVE SIME**

American Dave Sime was forced to miss the 100-meter dash at the 1956 Melbourne Olympics when he pulled a muscle. Four years later in Rome, Sime's rally fell inches short, and he finished second to Germany's Armin Hary.

9. ALAIN MIMOUN

French distance runner Alain Mimoun finished second behind the great Czech runner, Emil Zátopek, three times at the Olympics. He finally defeated his rival when he won the gold medal in the marathon at the 1956 Melbourne Olympics. He attributed his victory to wearing the number 13, which, contrary to popular belief, he considered lucky.

10. MARIA BRAUN

Maria Braun of Holland won the gold medal in the 100-meter backstroke at the 1928 Amsterdam Olympics. She was poised to swim for another gold medal at the 1932 Los Angeles Olympics when she developed blood poisoning from an insect bite and was unable to compete.

Fanatics

Spectators are an important part of the Olympic experience. Sometimes, they actually influence the outcome of competitions.

1. 1936 AUSTRIA VS. PERU SOCCER GAME

At the 1936 Berlin Olympics, the soccer game between Austria and Peru was disrupted by unruly fans. The match was tied 2–2 in the second overtime when a group of Peruvian spectators stormed the field and began attacking one of the Austrian players. With the spectators intimidating the Austrians, Peru scored two goals to win 4–2. The Austrians protested, and officials ordered the game replayed with no spectators. Peru refused and withdrew from the competition. Austria won the silver medal.

2. 1972 PAKISTAN FIELD HOCKEY

Germany defeated Pakistan 1–0 in the gold-medal game in field hockey at the 1972 Munich Olympics. Pakistan's supporters were so upset with the officiating that they rushed the judges' table and threw water in the face of René Frank, the president of the International Field Hockey Federation.

3. BEN ALVES

Uruguayan featherweight Ben Alves lost a controversial decision to American Eddie Johnson at the 1948 London Olympics. Outraged fans rioted for 20 minutes, but the decision was not overturned. Though Johnson won the controversial decision, he did not win a medal.

4. 1924 FRENCH RUGBY FANS

The United States humiliated France 17–3 in the gold-medal rugby game at the 1924 Paris Olympics. Two French players were injured during the roughly played contest. Unruly French fans began attacking Americans in the crowd. The American team received a police escort from the field. Rugby was discontinued as an Olympic sport following the Paris Games.

5. 1900 SWEDISH HAMMER THROWERS

The hammer-throw competition at the 1900 Paris Olympics was dominated by the Americans, who swept the top three places. The winner was John Flanagan. The main competition for the Americans came from a pair of inexperienced Swedish hammer throwers, Eric Lemming and Karl Staaf. The Swedes' throws were so erratic that spectators lining the field scattered to avoid being hit.

6. 1948 SWISS HOCKEY FANS

The hockey tournament at the 1948 St. Moritz Winter Olympics was marred by rowdy behavior by the Swiss spectators. During a game between Canada and Switzerland, the Swiss fans pelted officials with snowballs. Canada won the game 3–0 and went on to win the gold medal.

7. WLADYSLAW KOZAKIEWICZ

Spectators at the 1980 Moscow Olympics were among the worst-behaved in Olympic history. This was especially true at the pole-vault competition. They mercilessly booed foreign competitors. Most of their wrath was directed at Wladyslaw Kozakiewicz, who won the competition. After he clinched the gold medal, he showed what he thought of the crowd by making an obscene gesture.

8. WILLIAM SHERRING

Canadian William Sherring entered the stadium for his victory lap in the marathon at the 1906 Athens Olympics. Expecting to be cheered, Sherring instead was greeted by hostile shouts of "Xenos!" ("foreigner") by the Greek spectators, who had hoped that one of their runners would duplicate Spiridon Louis's triumph of 1896. Prince George graciously jogged with the winner for the final lap and helped avert a potentially ugly situation.

9. CARL LEWIS

Carl Lewis, winner of nine gold medals, was America's greatest Olympic athlete. When he competed in front of American fans at the 1984 Los Angeles Olympics, it should have been his greatest moment. In the long jump, Lewis soared 28 feet on his first attempt, virtually ensuring himself the gold medal. Lewis made one more jump and passed on the final four rounds to conserve energy for other events he had entered. Lewis was booed by many in the crowd who had hoped to see him break Bob Beamon's Olympic record. It was no way to treat an American hero.

10. **IRVING BAXTER**

American Irving Baxter set an Olympic record with a jump of
six feet, two inches in the high-jump competition at the 1900
Paris Olympics. Having won the competition, Baxter wanted
to attempt to break the world record of six feet, five inches.
Spectators, hoping to get a better view, crowded the jumping area. Distracted by the spectators, Baxter could not clear
the record height.

Olympic Oddballs

M eet some of the Olympics' most colorful characters.

1. **ALBERTO TOMBA**

Italian skier Alberto Tomba won gold medals at the 1988 and 1992 Winter Olympics, but he received just as much attention for his personal life. His father promised him a new Ferrari if he won a gold medal at the 1988 Calgary Olympics. Tomba won two gold medals and the red Ferrari.

At Calgary, Tomba arranged for a meeting with the beautiful women's Olympic figure skating gold medalist Katarina Witt. After winning her first gold medal at the 1984 Sarajevo Winter Olympics, Witt received 35,000 love letters from men around the world. Tomba was so smitten that he said, "If she does not win a gold medal, she can have one of mine."

The modest Tomba joked that Albertville, France, the site of the 1992 Winter Olympics, should be renamed Albertoville in his honor. He did win another gold medal in the giant slalom. When asked about his training regimen, Tomba replied, "I used to have a wild time with three women until

5 A.M., but I am getting older. In the Olympic village here, I will live it up with five women, but only until 3 A.M."

2. **UGO FRIGERO**

Ugo Frigero won gold medals in the 10,000-meter walk at the 1920 and 1924 Olympics. Frigero insisted that the band at the Olympic stadium play music when he entered. He gave the bandleader a list of selections. The Italian waved his arms to help the musicians keep the right tempo and once stopped during a race to yell instructions to the band.

3. **CASSIUS CLAY**

Light heavyweight Cassius Clay easily won the gold medal at the 1960 Rome Olympics. Clay, whose hand speed dazzled spectators, was just as quick with a quip. His witty banter earned him the nickname The Louisville Lip. Clay was so proud of his gold medal that he never took it off.

Upon returning home, he learned that not even his status as an Olympic champion could shield him from racism. An owner of a Louisville restaurant refused to serve Clay because he was an African-American. Afterwards, a motorcycle gang chased Clay and his friend, but, not surprisingly, the bikers came out on the short end of their fisticuffs with the boxing champion. Disillusioned, Clay threw his once-cherished gold medal off a bridge into the Ohio River. In 1964, Clay defeated Sonny Liston to win the heavyweight title and changed his name to Muhammad Ali. In 1996, Ali was presented with a replacement gold medal.

4. **MARJA-LILSA HAMALAINEN**

Marja-Lilsa Hamalainen won three gold medals in cross-country skiing events at the 1984 Sarajevo Winter Olympics.

The Finnish athlete was so publicity shy that she tried to run and hide from reporters after each victory. Only when she was cornered would she speak to journalists.

5. DIANA GORDON-LENNOX

Diana Gordon-Lennox finished twenty-ninth in the Alpine combined skiing competition at the Garmisch Winter Olympics. What made her achievement more notable is that she competed with an arm in a cast and used one pole. The eccentric Canadian also wore a monocle.

6. GLYNIS NUNN

In order to win a gold medal in the women's heptathlon at the 1984 Los Angeles Olympics, Glynis Nunn of Australia had to overcome a mental block. As a competitor in the 800-meter run, one of the heptathlon events, Nunn was unable to cross the "finish line" for the second time on the second lap. Only after receiving hypnosis was she able to run the race.

7. MARIELLE GOITSCHEL

Marielle Goitschel of France won a gold medal in the giant slalom at the 1964 Innsbruck Winter Olympics. At the press conference following her victory, she announced her engagement to the handsome star of the French ski team, Jean-Claude Killy. Many reporters printed the story before they realized that it was a hoax.

8. HO-JUN LI

Ho-Jun Li, a marksman from North Korea, won a gold medal in the small-bore-rifle prone-position competition at the 1972 Munich Olympics. When asked the secret of his success, he replied that he pretended that he was shooting at capitalists.

"Flo Jo"—Florence Griffith-Joyner—wows the crowd with her impeccable fashion sense at the 1988 Olympic trials.

9. **VALERIO ARRI**

Italian Valerio Arri won a bronze medal in the marathon at the 1920 Antwerp Olympics. Despite running 26 miles, Arri was so fresh that he did three cartwheels after crossing the finish line.

10. **FLORENCE GRIFFITH-JOYNER**

Florence Griffith-Joyner won three gold medals at the 1988 Seoul Olympics. The winner of the 100- and 200-meter dashes, she was almost as famous for her outfits. The attractive runner sometimes wore lacy outfits that she called "athletic negligees." She also painted each of her long fingernails a different color.

Mind Games

L et the mind games begin.

1. HASELY CRAWFORD

Hasely Crawford of Trinidad was a master at psyching out his opposition. At the 1976 Montreal Olympics, Crawford played mind games with other runners in the 100-meter sprint. One of his techniques was to intimidate other athletes by ranting. He recalled that he could look at some of them and tell that they were already defeated. Crawford won the gold medal in the 100-meter sprint in a time of 10.06 seconds.

2. BILL JOHNSON

Bill Johnson never lacked for confidence. Although no American man skier had ever medaled in an Olympic down-hill, Johnson remarked before the 1988 downhill at Sarajevo that everyone else was fighting for second place. Johnson backed up his boast with a gold-medal performance.

3. KATARINA WITT

Katarina Witt was always the center of attention at any skating event in which she competed. A dazzling combination of talent and beauty, she won Olympic gold medals in 1984 and 1988. Sometimes, to the delight of spectators, she skated to other competitors' music in practice. Her improvised routines often infuriated the other skaters, who felt she was showing off at their expense.

4. SHIRLEY BABASHOFF

Australian Shane Gould was expected to dominate the women's swimming competition at the 1972 Munich Olympics. Shirley Babashoff and other American swimmers wore T-shirts with the message, "All that glitters is not Gould." Gould did indeed glitter and won three gold medals.

5. GARY HALL, JR.

Prior to the swimming competition at the 2000 Sydney Olympics, American Gary Hall, Jr., said that the United States swimmers would "break the Australians like guitars." Hall had to eat his words when Ian Thorpe overtook Hall on the anchor leg of the 4×100-meter freestyle relay to give the Aussies a world record and a gold medal in an event traditionally won by the Americans. After the race, they mocked Hall by acting as though they were strumming guitars.

6. HENRI OREILLER

Frenchman Henri Oreiller was so confident that he was going to win the gold medal in the men's downhill at the 1948 St. Moritz Olympics that he told the other skiers that they were wasting their time. Oreiller proved a prophet as he won the race by more than four seconds.

Mildred "Babe" Didrikson of the United States in action with the javelin at the 1932 Olympic Games in Los Angeles, California.

7. **BABE DIDRIKSON**

Babe Didrikson won the javelin and 80-meter hurdles competitions at the 1932 Los Angeles Olympics. She irritated other athletes by boasting that she was going to "beat everyone in sight." Even more infuriating was that she usually did.

8. **EMIL ZÁTOPEK**

Emil Zátopek used his head as well as his legs to win races. The Czech star had never competed in a marathon prior to the 1952 Helsinki Olympics. Halfway through the race,

Zátopek ran beside Englishman Jim Peters, the favorite to win the gold medal. Zátopek asked, "I have not run in a marathon before. Don't you think we should run a bit faster?" Zátopek soon left the disheartened Peters behind and won the gold medal.

9. CORNELIUS JOHNSON

Cornelius Johnson was so confident that he was going to win the gold medal in the high jump at the 1936 Berlin Olympics that he did not even bother to remove his sweatsuit until the bar reached a height of six feet, six inches. Johnson cleared six feet, eight inches to win the gold medal.

10. MARIAN WORONIN

Polish sprinter Marian Woronin predicted before the 100-meter sprint at the 1980 Moscow Olympics that he would win the gold medal in a time of 10.1 seconds. The time would have won the gold medal. Unfortunately, Woronin finished seventh with a time of 10.46 seconds.

Bad Sports

Even great athletes sometimes can be poor sports.

1. MEYER PRINSTEIN

For religious reasons, American Meyer Prinstein refused to compete in the long jump at the 1900 Paris Olympics because it was scheduled on a Sunday. The winner of the competition was another American, Alvin Kraenzlein. Prinstein proposed that they have a jump-off the next day to determine the champion. When Kraenzlein declined, Prinstein punched him in the mouth. The feud between the two lasted for years. Prinstein won the gold medal in the long jump in both 1904 and 1908.

2. PAUL GRIFFIN

Irish featherweight Paul Griffin lost a match and his cool at the 1992 Barcelona Olympics. After being floored by Steven Chungu of Zambia, Griffin was enraged when the ring physician stopped the bout. Griffin had to be restrained from attacking the doctor.

3. **ROGER BROUSSE**

During a middleweight boxing match at the 1924 Paris Olympics, Frenchman Roger Brousse repeatedly bit his British opponent, Henry Mallin. The Englishman was appalled when it was announced that Brousse had won a close decision. The controversial decision was reversed when Mallin showed officials the bite marks on his chest. Mallin went on to win the gold medal.

4. **AMY VAN DYKEN**

American swimmer Amy Van Dyken was one of the stars of the 1996 Atlanta Olympics. She became the first American woman to win four gold medals in an Olympics. She was less successful at the 2000 Sydney Olympics. The sensation of the games was Inge de Bruijn. The Dutch swimmer won three gold medals in world-record time. Prior to the 50-meter freestyle final, Van Dyken, the defending Olympic champion, leaned over and spat in de Bruijn's lane. The ill-advised attempt to psych out de Bruijn backfired, as she won another gold medal and Van Dyken failed to win a medal.

5. **LAUNCESTON ELLIOT**

Launceston Elliot won a gold medal in weightlifting at the 1896 Athens Olympics. The British strongman also entered the super heavyweight Greco-Roman wrestling competition. When he lost to eventual champion Carl Schuhmann of Germany, Elliot insisted that his shoulders had not been pinned and refused to accept the decision. He had to be escorted away.

6. **LINFORD CHRISTIE**

The highlight of English sprinter Linford Christie's career was a gold medal in the 100-meter dash at the 1992 Barcelona Olympics. The low point of his career occurred four years later in the 100-meter sprint at the Atlanta Olympics. Christie was disqualified when he was charged with two false starts. In disbelief, Christie delayed the race by arguing with officials and refusing to leave the track. He showed his disgust by throwing his track shoes into a garbage can.

7. **NANCY KERRIGAN**

Figure skater Nancy Kerrigan won the sympathy of millions after she suffered a knee injury when she was attacked prior to the 1994 United States championship in Detroit. The assault had been planned by the husband of a rival skater, Tonya Harding. It appeared that there would be a storybook ending when Kerrigan skated a near-perfect performance at the 1994 Winter Olympics. Her dream of a gold medal was shattered when Oksana Baiul of the Ukraine skated a flawless routine to narrowly defeat her. The emotional Baiul seemed to be always in tears, and Kerrigan's frustration got the best of her. When Baiul was late for the medal ceremony, Kerrigan commented that Baiul would probably just cry anyway.

8. **DAVID RIGERT**

David Rigert of the Soviet Union was favored to win the middle heavyweight weightlifting division at the 1972 Munich Olympics. He lost control when he bombed out and failed to medal. Rigert shocked onlookers by hitting his head against a wall and pulling out fistfuls of his hair. Four years later, at the Munich Olympics, Rigert won the gold medal.

9. DAVID HUNT AND ALAN WARREN

David Hunt and Alan Warren of Great Britain won silver medals in the tempest sailing class at the 1972 Munich Olympics. When they failed to win a medal at the 1976 Munich Olympics, Hunt and Warren set their boat on fire.

10. SCOTT LEARY

The men's 50-yard freestyle swimming competition at the 1904 St. Louis Olympics was filled with controversy. It appeared that Hungarian Zoltán Halmaj had won, but a judge from the United States declared that an American swimmer, Scott Leary, was the winner. The decision caused a near riot. Adding to the confusion was Leary's claim that Halmaj had held him back near the finish line. It was decided that the matter should be decided by a swim-off. This time Halmaj clearly won.

Unlikely Champions

Nothing of these Olympic champions were expected to win a gold medal.

1. EDGAR AAYBE

Edgar Aaybe was a Danish journalist covering the 1900 Paris Olympics. In the tug-of-war competition, the team represented by athletes from Denmark and Sweden needed another man and asked Aaybe if he would join. They won the competition, and Aaybe became an improbable Olympic champion.

2. MICHELINE OSTERMEYER

One of the most unlikely Olympic athletes was Micheline Ostermeyer of France. A few months before she competed in the 1948 London Olympics, Ostermeyer graduated from the renowned Paris Conservatory of Music. The French track and field team needed a discus thrower, and although she had competed in the event only one time, Ostermeyer agreed to try. Ostermeyer not only won a gold medal in the discus, but she also won gold in her specialty, the shot put. Following her athletic career, Ostermeyer became a concert pianist.

3. PAUL PILGRIM

Paul Pilgrim did not make the 1906 United States Olympic team. When he decided to pay his own way to Athens, he was permitted to compete in the 400- and 800-meter runs. Pilgrim, who had never won a major international competition, won gold medals in both races.

4. BOB GARRETT

Bob Garrett was America's best shot putter at the 1896 Athens Olympics. When he arrived in Athens, Garrett picked up a discus that was lying in the grass. After throwing it a couple of times, Garrett decided to enter the event. Garrett won both the discus and shot-put competition.

5. JOSIA THUGWANE

Less than six months before he was to compete in the marathon at the 1996 Atlanta Olympics, South African runner Josia Thugwane was shot in the chin during a carjacking. Thugwane not only survived the shooting, he won the gold medal. He was so naïve about the Olympics that he was not aware that there was a medal ceremony after the event.

6. WALDEMAR CIERPINSKI

American Frank Shorter won the gold medal in the marathon at the 1972 Olympics. He appeared to be on his way to a second gold medal at the 1976 Munich Olympics when another runner joined him at the front of the pack. Shorter had no idea who the obscure runner was. It turned out to be Waldemar Cierpinksi of the German Democratic

Republic, and he defeated Shorter by 50 seconds to win the gold medal. Cierpinski proved his victory was no fluke by winning the marathon at the 1980 Moscow Olympics.

7. ANTHONY NASH AND ROBIN DIXON

Anthony Nash and Robin Dixon of Great Britain won the gold medal in the two-man bobsled competition at the 1964 Innsbruck Olympics. What made the achievement so outstanding was that there were no bobsled runs in Great Britain at the time.

8. MARC ROSSET

The men's field in the tennis competition at the 1992 Barcelona Olympics was a virtual who's who of tennis stars. Favorites included Pete Sampras, Stefan Edberg, Boris Becker, Jim Courier, and Michael Chang. Incredibly, none of these champions even medaled. The surprise gold medalist was Marc Rosset of Switzerland. He defeated another little-known player, Jordi Arresse of Spain, 7−6, 6−4, 3−6, 4−6, 8−6 in the final.

9. TRENT DIMAS

American gymnast Trent Dimas finished only sixth in the qualifying round for the horizantal-bar competition at the 1992 Barcelona Olympics. Not expected to win a medal, Dimas was a surprise gold medalist.

10. ÁGNES KELETI

Women's gymnastic competitions have been dominated in recent Olympics by teenagers. In 1956, thirty-five-year-old Ágnes Keleti of Hungary won gold medals in the floor exercise, balance beam, and uneven bars.

Billy Mills won a major upset, taking gold in the 10,000-meter run at the 1964 Tokyo games.

Ultimate Upsets

These athletes pulled off some of the biggest upsets in Olympic history.

1. BILLY MILLS

No one expected American Billy Mills to win a medal in the 10,000-meter run at the 1964 Tokyo Olympics. Mills did not even win his race at the United States Olympic trials. With one lap to go, it appeared he was out of contention for the gold medal, but Mills unleashed a powerful kick and passed Australia's Ron Clarke and Tunisia's Mohammed Gammoudi to win. Mills had run the race of his life. His time was 46 seconds faster than his previous personal best. Mills was so unknown that after the race an official asked him, "Who are you?" Ron Clarke, the pre-race favorite, admitted he had never heard of Mills.

2. RULON GARDNER

Super heavyweight Greco-Roman wrestler Aleksandr Karelin was considered unbeatable entering the 2000 Sydney

Olympics. The Russian had won the previous three gold medals and had never lost a match in 13 years of international competition. By contrast, American Rulon Gardner had never medaled at a world competition. Karelin and Gardner met in the gold-medal match at Sydney. In their previous match, Karelin had defeated Gardner easily by the score of 7−0. Gardner beat Karelin 1−0 in the biggest upset of the 2000 Sydney Olympics.

3. 1980 U.S. HOCKEY TEAM

The Soviet hockey team was a heavy favorite to win its fifth consecutive gold medal at the 1980 Lake Placid Winter Olympics. The United States hockey team had not won a gold medal since a surprise triumph at the 1960 Lake Placid Winter Olympics. The Americans had been humiliated by the Russians 10−3 in a pre-Olympic exhibition game. They met again in the semifinal game at Lake Placid. Mike Eruzione's third-period goal gave the Americans a shocking 4−3 victory. Two days later, the United States defeated Finland 4−2 to win. Announcer Al Michaels summed up the achievement when he asked television viewers, "Do you believe in miracles?"

4. PERCY WILLIAMS

Percy Williams of Canada was an unexpected winner of the 100-meter dash at the 1928 Amsterdam Olympics. That evening, a crowd of Canadian supporters stood outside Williams's hotel, hoping to catch a glimpse of their new national hero. Williams was such an unknown that he stood unnoticed in the crowd waiting for himself to appear.

5. JOSEF BARTHEL

Roger Bannister, the Englishman who in 1954 became the first man to run a sub-four-minute mile, was a favorite to win the gold medal in the 1,500-meter run at the 1952 Helsinki Olympics. Bannister proved a disappointment by finishing fourth. The winner was Josef Barthel from the tiny European country of Luxembourg.

6. ANDRE PHILLIPS

Edwin Moses, the 1976 and 1984 gold medalist in the 400-meter hurdles, won 107 consecutive races between 1977 and 1987. He was an overwhelming favorite to win another gold medal at the 1988 Seoul Olympics. The best Moses could do was a bronze medal. The winner was another American, Andre Phillips. Prior to his gold-medal performance, Phillips had raced against Moses more than 20 times without a single victory.

7. KONSTADÍNOS KEDÉRIS

Konstadínos Kedéris of Greece won the gold medal in the 200-meter sprint at the 2000 Sydney Games. He was so obscure that Michael Johnson, the 1996 200-meter gold medalist, admitted that he had never heard of Kedéris.

8. FRANCISCO FERNANDEZ-OCHOA

Francisco Fernandez-Ochoa won Spain's first-ever gold medal at a Winter Olympics when he finished first in the slalom at the 1972 Sapporo Games. Before his Olympic victory, Ochoa's best finish in an international competition was sixth.

9. ALLEN WOODRING

Allen Woodring was not expected to compete in the 200-meter dash at the 1920 Antwerp Olympics. An alternate, he was only able to participate when another American runner, George Massengale, was injured. Woodring outran teammate Charley Paddock to win the gold medal. He was so surprised by his victory that he believed that Paddock, the 100-meter gold medalist, had let him win.

10. 1960 PAKISTAN FIELD HOCKEY TEAM

India is not exactly an Olympic powerhouse, but its field hockey team dominated the event from 1928 to 1960. They won 30 games in a row, outscoring their opponents 197–8. The streak ended in the 1960 Rome Olympics when Pakistan defeated India 1–0 in the gold-medal game.

They Should Have Won the Gold Medal

Sometimes circumstances beyond an athlete's control can derail dreams of Olympic glory.

1. EDWIN MOSES

Edwin Moses won the gold medal in the 400-meter hurdles at the 1976 Montreal Olympics. He was the favorite to win his specialty at the 1980 Moscow Olympics but was not able to compete because of the U.S. boycott of the Games. Moses won a second gold medal in the 400-meter hurdles at the 1984 Olympics in Los Angeles.

2. MICHAEL JOHNSON

Michael Johnson was a prohibitive favorite to win the gold medal in the 200-meter run at the 1992 Barcelona Olympics. In Spain, Johnson contracted food poisoning. The illness weakened him and disrupted his training. He was eliminated in the semifinal heat. Four years later, Johnson set a world record in winning the 200-meter gold medal at Atlanta.

3. **MARY T. MEAGHER**

One of the athletes most penalized by the American boycott of the 1980 Moscow Olympics was swimmer Mary T. Meagher. The world record holder in both the 100- and 200-meter butterfly, she was denied the opportunity to win two gold medals. At the 1984 Los Angeles Olympics, Meagher won gold medals in both events.

4. **JAMES CARLTON**

Australian James Carlton was the co-holder of the world record in the 200-meter dash. He was expected to challenge for the gold medal at the 1932 Los Angeles Olympics, but just before the Games began, Carlton retired from track and field, became a monk, and entered a monastery.

5. **SERGEI BUBKA**

Sergei Bubka of the Soviet Union was the world record holder in the pole vault and the favorite to win his first gold medal at the 1984 Los Angeles Olympics. Unfortunately, the Soviet Union boycotted the 1984 games, and Bubka had to wait until 1988 to claim his first gold medal. Three years later, he became the first pole vaulter to clear a height of 20 feet.

6. **ANA QUIROT**

Cuban Ana Quirot ran in more than a dozen 800-meter races in 1988 and was undefeated. Quirot probably would have won a gold medal at the 1988 Seoul Olympics, but she was not allowed to compete because Cuba was one of the nations boycotting the Games. She won a bronze medal in the 800-meters in 1992 and a silver in 1996.

7. YELENA MUKHINA

Two weeks before she was to compete in the 1980 Moscow Games, Soviet gymnast Yelena Mukhina, the reigning world champion, fell in a practice exercise and fractured her spine. The injury left her paralyzed from the neck down.

8. STANLEY FLOYD

Stanley Floyd won the 100-meter sprint in the 1980 Olympic trials and hoped to become the first American gold medalist in the event since Jim Hines in 1968. His Olympic dreams were shattered when President Jimmy Carter announced a U.S. boycott of the Moscow Games. Floyd's Olympic trial time was nearly two-tenths of a second faster than Moscow gold medalist Allan Wells of Great Britain.

9. MARTY GLICKMAN AND SAM STOLLER

Marty Glickman and Sam Stoller were the only Jewish athletes on the 1936 United States Olympic track team. They were scheduled to compete on the highly favored American 4×100-meter relay team. At the last minute, Glickman and Stoller were replaced by Jesse Owens and Ralph Metcalfe, the gold and silver medalists in the 100-meter dash. Glickman and Stoller were told the change was made to give the United States a better chance to win the gold medal. However, many thought the switch had been made to appease Adolf Hitler, who was hosting the 1936 Berlin Games.

10. **WALTER DRAY**

Walter Dray, the world record holder in the pole vault, did not compete in the 1908 London Olympics. The reason for his absence was that his mother thought he was jumping too high and might be injured if he competed.

They Never Won Gold

S ome of the world's greatest athletes have competed in the Olympics and left without a gold medal.

1. JIM RYUN

Jim Ryun was one of the greatest middle-distance runners in track history. At the 1968 Mexico City Olympics, Ryun finished second in the 1,500 meters to Kip Keino, a runner from Kenya who had never defeated him. Ryun attempted to avenge the defeat in the 1,500 meters at the 1972 Munich Olympics. In a preliminary heat, Ryun fell and lay stunned on the track for eight seconds. He courageously tried to catch the pack but was unable to qualify for the final.

2. MARY DECKER SLANEY

Few athletes had more frustrating Olympic careers than Mary Decker Slaney. The greatest woman middle-distance runner in American track history, Slaney's Olympic career was marred by injuries and disappointments. She missed the 1980 Moscow Games because of the U.S. boycott. Her frustration was exemplified at the 1984 Los Angeles Olympics.

Mary Decker Slaney struggles with the agony of defeat after her infamous accidental clash with Zola Budd at the 1984 Los Angeles Olympics.

Slaney was in position to win her first gold medal when she tripped over the heels of South African Zola Budd and fell. Writhing in pain, Slaney could not continue. In the 1988 Seoul Olympics, Slaney finished a disappointing eighth in the 1,500-meter race. She led the 3,000-meter race only to fade and finish tenth. Slaney gave it a final try at the 1996 Atlanta Olympics. Past her prime, she was eliminated in the first round of the 5,000-meter run.

3. RON CLARKE

Australian Ron Clarke set nearly 20 world records during his track career. At the 1964 and 1968 Olympics, Clarke competed in six distance races and came away with only a bronze medal. While Clarke never won a gold medal, he did receive one. The great Czech runner Emil Zátopek, winner of four Olympic gold medals, gave Clarke one of his in recognition of Clarke's brilliant career.

4. GRETE WAITZ

Grete Waitz of Norway helped popularize women's distance running by winning races around the world. The Olympic women's marathon was held for the first time in the 1984 Los Angeles Games. Waitz had never lost a marathon and was expected to win. She finished second, 1 minute, 26 seconds behind Joan Benoit.

5. GLENN CUNNINGHAM

Glenn Cunningham suffered serious burns on his legs in a schoolhouse fire when he was eight years old. Cunningham not only regained the use of his legs, but he became one of the world's best middle-distance runners. Cunningham finished fourth in the 1,500-meter run at the 1932 Los Angeles

Olympics after winning a silver medal in the race at the 1936 Berlin Games.

6. MERLEΠE OTTEY

Merlene Ottey of Jamaica won seven Olympic medals in sprint races between 1980 and 1996. At the 1996 Atlanta Olympics, Ottey won silver medals in the 100- and 200-meter races. She finished her career with two silver and five bronze medals, but no gold.

7. MARIA WALLISER

Swiss skier Maria Walliser was a world champion during the 1980s. Beautiful and talented, she had everything but an Olympic gold medal. Walliser nearly won in the women's downhill at the 1984 Sarajevo Olympics, finishing five-hundredths of a second behind another Swiss skier, Michela Figini. Four years later, at Calgary, Walliser won bronze medals in the giant slalom and alpine combined.

8. FILBERT BAYI

Tanzania's Filbert Bayi was forced to miss the 1976 Montreal Olympics because of the boycott by African nations. The boycott cost Bayi a chance at a gold medal. The winning time in the 1,500-meter race was almost seven seconds slower than Bayi's world record. Bayi did win a silver medal in the 3,000-meter steeplechase at the 1980 Moscow Olympics.

9. EAMONN COGHLAN

Ireland's Eamonn Coghlan was one of the most accomplished middle-distance runners in the world during the 1970s and 1980s. Coghlan led the 1,500-meter run at the

1976 Montreal Olympics before weakening to finish fourth. Coghlan also competed in the 1980 and 1988 Olympics but never won a medal.

10. **STEVE PREFONTAINE**

Steve Prefontaine was a charismatic athlete who dominated American middle-distance running in the early 1970s. In Munich, at the 1972 Olympics, Prefontaine led late in the race but faded to finish fourth. Prefontaine's promising career ended in 1975 when the 24-year-old was killed in an automobile accident.

Forgotten Gold

You may have never heard of these athletes, but they all were multiple gold winners.

1. RAISA SMETANINA

Raisa Smetanina won ten Olympic medals in Nordic skiing. The Soviet cross-country skier won gold medals in the ten-kilometer race at the 1976 Innsbruck Winter Olympics and in the five-kilometer race at Lake Placid in 1980.

2. MARTIN SHERIDAN

One of America's earliest Olympic heroes, Martin Sheridan won nine medals, five of them gold. Sheridan won the discus competition at the 1904, 1906, and 1908 Olympics.

3. VILHO RITOLA

Not nearly as famous as his countryman Paavo Nurmi, Finland's Vilho Ritola won five gold medals during his track career. In the 5,000-meter race at the 1928 Amsterdam Olympics, Ritola defeated Nurmi by two seconds.

4. ANTON HEIDA

Anton Heida may not be the most famous American gymnast, but he was one of the most successful. At the 1904 St. Louis Olympics, Heida won five gold medals, including the horizontal bar and pommel horse competition.

5. A. CLAS THUNBERG

A. Clas Thunberg won five gold medals in speed skating. The Finnish skater won three at the 1924 Chamonix Winter Olympics and two more at St. Moritz in 1928.

6. NEDO NADI

Italian fencer Nedo Nadi won five gold medals at the 1920 Antwerp Olympics. Nadi won both the individual sabre and foil.

7. SIXTEN JERNBERG

Sweden's Sixten Jernberg racked up nine Olympic medals in Nordic skiing between 1956 and 1964. He won four gold medals, three silver, and two bronze. Jernberg won the grueling 50-kilometer cross-country race in 1956 and 1964.

8. GEORGES MIEZ

Swiss gymnast Georges Miez won three gold medals at the 1928 Amsterdam Olympics. Miez competed in the Olympics between 1924 and 1936 and collected four gold medals and eight medals total.

9. MARCUS HURLEY

American Marcus Hurley was the cycling star of the 1904 St. Louis Olympics. He won gold medals in the quarter-mile, third-mile, half-mile, and mile races. All of these cycling races were held only at the 1904 Games.

10. GEORGE EYSER

American gymnast George Eyser won three gold, two silver, and one bronze medal at the 1904 St. Louis Olympics. His gold medals came in the parallel bars and vault.

Queens of the Ice

The most popular event of the Winter Olympics is usually the women's figure skating competition. Ice queens such as Sonja Henie, Carol Heiss, Dorothy Hamill, Katarina Witt, and Tara Lipinski have all won Olympic gold. However, not all great women skaters have stood atop the Olympic podium.

1. JANET LYNN

Janet Lynn is often called the greatest skater who ever lived. Dick Button described her skating as being like "one smooth flowing thread of silk." No skater expressed the joy of skating better than the tiny girl from Rockford, Illinois. From 1969 to 1973, she reigned as United States figure skating champion. Despite frequently earning perfect scores of 6.0 for her free skating, she never won a world championship. When she failed to win at the 1971 world championship in Lyon, France, the angry crowd nearly caused a riot. Her weakness was school figures, and it cost her the gold medal at the 1972 Sapporo Winter Olympics. Beatrix Schuba of Austria was one of the best school-figures skaters in history and built an insurmountable lead. Although Lynn won the free skate and Schuba was seventh, Lynn was awarded the bronze medal. The furor over the outcome was a primary reason that a short program was added the next year at the world championship to make it easier for superior free skaters to win.

2. **TONYA HARDING**

Just like Janet Lynn, Tonya Harding never won a world championship, but her impact on figure skating was enormous. At the 1991 United States figure skating championship, Harding became the first American woman to land a triple axel—a three-and-a-half revolution jump—and won her only national title. Harding finished fourth at the 1992 Albertville Winter Olympics. She set her sights on the 1994 Lillehammer Winter Games. The women's competition became a media circus when it was learned that Harding's husband had planned the attack that injured her principal rival, Nancy Kerrigan. Harding skated below par and finished eighth, but the Olympic women's figure skating competition was the fourth most-watched program in television history. After the Olympics, Harding pleaded guilty to hindering her husband's prosecution and resigned from the United States Figure Skating Association.

3. **DENISE BIELLMANN**

Swiss skater Denise Biellmann was one of the greatest jumpers and spinners in figure skating history. She was the first woman to land a triple lutz in competition, and she invented the Biellmann spin, in which she reached back and pulled her leg over her head. Biellmann won the free skating portion at the 1980 Lake Placid Olympics, but her twelfth-place finish in the school figures kept her off the medal stand. Biellmann won the world championship the next year and turned professional.

4. **MIDORI ITO**

Midori Ito of Japan was the first woman skater to land the triple axel jump. Ito won the 1989 world championship. A tenth-place finish in school figures dropped her from medal contention at the 1988 Calgary Olympics. Ito skated well at the 1992 Albertville Games but finished second to American Kristi Yamaguchi.

5. **JILL TRENARY**

Jill Trenary was known for her well-choreographed routines. Trenary won three national championships and was the world champion in 1990. Trenary had a disappointing fourth-place finish at the 1988 Calgary Winter Olympics.

6. **NANCY KERRIGAN**

Nancy Kerrigan was the women's champion at the 1993 United States figure skating championship. She won a bronze medal at the 1992 Albertville Winter Olympics. Kerrigan skated brilliantly at the 1994 Lillehammer Olympics but narrowly lost the gold medal to Oksana Baiul of the Ukraine.

7. **ROSALYNN SUMNERS**

A three-time national champion, Rosalynn Sumners was also the 1983 world champion. The American finished second at the 1984 Sarajevo Winter Olympics when the judges split 5–4 in favor of Katarina Witt.

8. LINDA FRATIANNE

American Linda Fratianne is remembered as one of the first women skaters to land multiple triple jumps in a program. She was a four-time national champion and won the world championship in 1977 and 1979. At the 1980 Lake Placid Winter Olympics, she finished second behind East German Anett Pötzsch. When she returned home, Fratianne expressed her disappointment by wrapping her silver medal in toilet paper and storing it under her bed for more than a decade.

9. ELAINE ZAYAK

Elaine Zayak lost three toes in a lawn mower accident as a child. She overcame her injury and developed into a tremendous jumper. Zayak won the 1981 U.S. championship and 1982 world championship with an arsenal of triple jumps. She lost all chance for a medal at the 1984 Sarajevo Winter Olympics when she finished thirteenth in compulsory figures. Zayak finished sixth in the competition.

10. JILL SAWYER

Before Tonya Harding, Jill Sawyer was the greatest jumper in the history of American women's figure skating. During the late 1970s, Sawyer was landing jumps that only Denise Biellmann could match. Sawyer won the national novice and junior championships and seemed poised to eventually win national and world titles until an automobile accident derailed her career. Her coach, Carlo Fassi, the man who trained Olympic champions Peggy Fleming, Dorothy Hamill, and John Curry, said that Sawyer should have won two Olympic gold medals.

The Olympics' Most Embarrassing Moments

For every moment of Olympic glory, there's a moment an athlete would rather forget.

1. JOSEPH GUILLEMOT

The starting time for the 10,000-meter run at the 1920 Antwerp Olympics was moved up three hours at the request of the King of Belgium. This was bad news for French runner Joseph Guillemot, who had just eaten a large meal. Guillemot still managed to run well, finishing second behind rival Paavo Nurmi. Nauseated, Guillemot vomited on Nurmi's shoes after crossing the finish line.

2. LASSE VIREN

Lasse Viren of Finland won gold medals in both the 5,000- and 10,000-meter runs at the 1972 and 1976 Olympics. Viren's attempt to win the marathon in the 1980 Moscow Olympics was less successful. Struck with an attack of diarrhea during the race, he had to run off the course and into the bushes when nature called. He was forced to drop out of the race a few miles later.

3. ELVIRA OZOLINA

Elvira Ozolina of the Soviet Union won the gold medal in the women's javelin throw at the 1960 Rome Olympics. She was so humiliated with her fifth-place finish at the 1964 Tokyo games that she shaved her head.

4. ALEKSANDR BORTYUK

Aleksandr Bortyuk of the Soviet Union made a crucial mistake at the beginning of a run during the four-man bobsled competition at the 1992 Albertville Winter Olympics. Bortyuk slipped on the ice and fell into the bobsled facing the wrong way. His team did not win a medal.

5. ALEXANDRA SCHREIBER

Alexandra Schreiber of Germany suffered a humiliating defeat in the middleweight judo competition at the 1992 Barcelona Olympics. She was beaten in seven seconds by Italy's Emanuela Pierantozzi.

6. INGEMAR JOHANSSON

Ingemar Johansson knocked out Floyd Patterson in 1959 to become heavyweight boxing champion of the world. Johansson had competed in the heavyweight boxing competition at the 1952 Helsinki Olympics. In the gold-medal match against American Ed Sanders, the Swede backpedaled, covered up, and barely threw a punch. He was disqualified in the second round for passivity. The performance was so shameful that Johansson was not given his silver medal until 1981.

7. ANTONIUS LEMBERKOVITS

At the small-bore-rifle competition at the 1932 Lake Placid Olympics, Hungarian Antonius Lemberkovits made a bull's-eye. Unfortunately, he had aimed at the wrong target. The miss cost him a chance to win the gold medal.

8. RANDY BARNES

During the warm-up for the men's shot-put competition at the 1996 Atlanta Olympics, Randy Barnes was hit in the back by a throw made by teammate John Godina as Barnes attempted to retrieve his shot put. Luckily, he was not injured and went on to win the gold medal. Godina won the silver medal.

9. HANS-JÜRGEN TODT

Hans-Jürgen Todt of West Germany let his temper get the best of him in the pentathlon competition at the 1968 Mexico City Olympics. When his horse balked three times at one of the jumps, Todt began attacking the animal and had to be restrained.

10. ERIKA SALUMÄE

It was a proud moment for Erika Salumäe of Estonia when she won a gold medal in the 1,000-meter match sprint cycling race at the 1992 Barcelona Olympics. Spanish officials turned it into an awkward moment when they raised the Estonian flag upside-down at the medals ceremony.

Biggest Blunders

Sometimes Olympic athletes make mistakes of judgment that cost them medals.

1. EDDIE HART AND REY ROBINSON

A scheduling error cost American sprinters Eddie Hart and Rey Robinson a chance to win medals in the 100-meter dash at the 1972 Munich Olympics. Their coach, Stan Wright, had an outdated schedule for the qualifying heats. As a result, Hart and Robinson, who had each won their first heat, missed the second heat and did not qualify for the finals.

2. MIRUTS YIFTER

Miruts Yifter of Ethiopia missed his qualifying heat for the 5,000-meter run at the 1972 Munich Olympics. Why Yifter missed the heat has remained a mystery, although stories suggest that he spent too long in the bathroom or that he got lost on the way to the track. Yifter made up for his mistake by winning the gold medal in the 5,000 meters at the 1980 Moscow Olympics.

3. GILLIS GRAFSTRÖM

Sweden's Gillis Grafström won gold medals in men's figure skating at the 1920, 1924, and 1928 Olympics. Grafström lost his chance to win a fourth consecutive gold medal at the 1932 Lake Placid Winter Olmpics when he mistakenly traced the wrong figure. Grafström's blunder dropped him to second place behind Karl Schafer of Austria.

4. ILSE DÖRFFELDT

The German team had a ten-meter lead going into the final handoff of the women's 4×100-meter relay at the 1936 Berlin Olympics. As Marie Dollinger passed the baton to Ilse Dörffeldt, Dörffeldt dropped it. The American team went on to win the gold medals while the Germans watched in tears.

5. PEDRO VALLANA

Pedro Vallana led his Spanish soccer team to a silver medal at the 1920 Antwerp Olympics, but Vallana turned from hero to goat at the 1924 Paris Games. He accidentally kicked the ball into his own net in a 1–0 loss to Italy. Spain did not medal in soccer in 1924.

6. JOSEF VOJTA

Czechoslovakia and Hungary met in the gold-medal soccer game at the 1964 Tokyo Olympics. Hungary's first goal of the game was inadvertently deflected into the net by Czechoslovakia's Josef Vojta. The blunder proved decisive as Hungary won 2–1.

7. SUSAN PLATT

Susan Platt of Great Britain threw the javelin 177 feet on her third attempt at the 1960 Rome Olympics. The throw was ten feet farther than her longest previous throw and would have been long enough to win a silver medal. Platt tried to get a better look at where it landed, but unfortunately, she stepped over the line and the throw was nullified by the foul.

8. LOREN MURCHISON

A misunderstanding cost American sprinter Loren Murchison a chance at a medal in the 100-meter dash at the 1920 Antwerp Olympics. In the finals, Murchison misunderstood the starter's instructions, which were given in French. Instead of getting into a set stance, Murchison stood up. He was left behind when the gun went off and finished last.

9. WIM ESSAJAS

Wim Essajas was the only member of the Surinam team at the 1960 Rome Olympics. The first athlete to represent the tiny South American country, Essajas was scheduled to run in the 800-meter race. Misinformed about the starting time for his qualifying heat, he overslept and missed his chance to compete in the Olympics.

10. 1896 AMERICAN OLYMPIC TEAM

The 1896 American team almost arrived too late to compete in the Athens Olympics. Unaware that the Greek calendar was different from their own, the athletes believed they were actually 12 days early.

Worst Performances

The Jamaican bobsled team gained notoriety for its dismal performances at the Winter Olympics. In fact, all of the following athletes performed much more poorly.

1. ERIC MOUSSAMBANI

Eric Moussambani showed why Equitorial Guinea is not considered a powerhouse in Olympic swimming. Moussambani competed in the 100-meter freestyle at the 2000 Sydney Olympics. In his qualifying heat, Moussambani did the dog paddle as he struggled to finish the race. He struggled so much that a radio announcer almost jumped into the pool because he thought Moussambani was drowning. His final time of 1 minute and 52 seconds was more than a minute slower than the winning time. Journalists gave him the nickname Eric the Eel.

2. ROBERTO ALVAREZ

Mexico has never been a medal threat at the Winter Olympics. Roberto Alvarez was Mexico's hope in the 50-kilometer Nordic skiing competition at the 1988 Calgary Winter

Games. Alvarez finished nearly an hour behind the next-to-last finisher. He was so far behind that worried officials sent out a search party to see if he had been injured.

3. **ANTOIN MILIORDOS**

The most pathetic skiing performance in Olympic history was turned in by Antoin Miliordos of Greece. In the men's slalom at the 1952 Oslo Winter Olympics, Miliordos fell 18 times and sat down in the middle of his run. He crossed the finish line facing backwards. His time for one run was 27 seconds slower than the winner's combined two-run time.

4. **RESAT ERCES**

Turkish skier Resat Erces set records for futility at the 1936 Winter Olympics that may never be equaled. The Alpine combined competition required skiers to complete a downhill and two slalom runs. Erces took more than 22 minutes to finish the downhill course, 18 minutes slower than the best time. Erces averaged five miles per hour during his downhill. Erces also competed in the 4×10-kilometer cross-country and recorded the slowest relay leg in Winter Olympic history.

5. **KYUNG SOON-YIM**

It was not surprising that Kyung Soon-Yim finished last in the men's slalom at the 1960 Squaw Valley Winter Olympics. He had practiced on grass, never skied on snow prior to the Olympics, and learned to ski by reading instructional books.

6. **THE 1920 CZECH HOCKEY TEAM**

Czechoslovakia's hockey team at the 1920 Antwerp Olympics won a bronze medal despite being outscored in the tournament 31 goals to 1. The Czechs lost to Canada 15–0 and were beaten by the United States 16–0. Somehow, they defeated Sweden 1–0 to clinch the bronze medal.

7. OLMEUS CHARLES

The Haitian track team at the 1976 Montreal Olympics was one of the worst in Olympic history. It was reported that Haitian dictator "Baby Doc" Duvalier had hand-selected the team without conducting Olympic trials. In the 10,000-meter qualifying heat, Olmeus Charles ran the slowest time in Olympic history.

8. RAYMOND KAYROUZ

Skiers competing in the giant slalom at the 1992 Albertville Winter Olympics were sent down the course in 40-second intervals. Raymond Kayrouz of Lebanon was so slow that he was actually passed by another skier, El Hassan Matha of Morocco.

9. GEORGE LISTER

The slowest marathon in Olympic history was run by George Lister of Canada in 1908. His time of 4:22:45 was almost an hour and a half slower than the winning time.

10. VICTOR ARBEZ

The biathlon combines cross-country skiing and shooting. In the 20-kilometer biathlon at the 1960 Squaw Valley Winter Olympics, Frenchman Victor Arbez was fastest in the skiing portion but missed 18 of 20 targets to finish last in the shooting phase and out of medal competition.

Unusual Awards

The gold medal was not presented to Olympic champions until the 1904 St. Louis Olympics. Before that, winners were presented with silver medals, a diploma, and a crown of olive branches. The second-place finisher was given a bronze medal and a crown of laurel. Olympic champions sometimes received other awards in addition to their medals. Billy Sherring, the 1906 marathon winner, was presented with a lamb and a three-foot-high statue of Athena. Each of the winners at the 1936 Berlin Olympics received a potted oak seedling.

1. SPIRIDON LOUIS

Spiridon Louis won the marathon at the 1896 Athens Olympics. The Greek runner was showered with gifts by his appreciative countrymen. As Louis neared the finish line, spectators threw money, jewelry, flowers, and hats at his feet in tribute. Following his victory, Louis was offered underwear, meals, and free shoeshines and shaves for life. A female admirer sent him a watch studded with pearls. Louis, a farmer, asked for only a cart to help him carry water.

2. SOMLUCK KAMSING

Featherweight boxer Somluck Kamsing won Thailand's first gold medal at the 1996 Atlanta Olympics. Upon arrival home, Kamsing was given more than a million dollars by the government and Olympic sponsors.

3. TAKANOBU JUMONJI

Takanobu Jumonji of Japan won a bronze medal in the 1,000-meter time trial at the 1996 Atlanta Olympics. Although Jumonji did not win the gold medal, he was given more than 40 million yen upon his return by organizations attempting to promote cycling in Japan. The award equated to nearly $400,000.

4. ALLAN KUSUMA AND SUSI SUSANTI

Badminton may not be a major sport in most countries, but it is in Indonesia. At the 1992 Barcelona Olympics, Allan Kusuma won the gold medal in men's singles and Susi Susanti won the gold in women's singles. National heroes in Indonesia, each received more than $200,000 for their Olympic victories.

5. SAID AOUITA

Said Aouita of Morocco won the gold medal in the 5,000-meter run at the 1984 Los Angeles Olympics. King Hassan II expressed his appreciation by presenting Aouita with a villa in Casablanca.

6. JEFFERSON PEREZ QUEZADA

Jefferson Perez Quezada won the gold medal in the 20-kilometer walk at the 1996 Atlanta Olympics. Quezada became the first Olympic medalist from Ecuador. One of the gifts that he received at home was a lifetime supply of yogurt.

7. SHUHEI NISHIDA AND SUEO OE

Japanese pole vaulters Shuhei Nishida and Sueo Oe tied for the second-best height cleared at the 1936 Berlin Olympics. When the two men declined to compete in a jump-off, it was decided to award the silver medal to Nishida and the bronze to Oe. The two friends decided to have their medals cut in half and soldered together so that each man had a medal that was half silver and half bronze.

8. BARBARA ANN SCOTT

Before leaving to compete at the 1948 St. Moritz Winter Olympics, figure skater Barbara Ann Scott was presented with a yellow convertible by her hometown of Ottawa. Olympic officials threatened to strip Scott of her amateur status if she accepted the car. She returned the gift and went on to win the gold medal. After the Olympics, she turned professional and got to keep the car for good.

9. ABEBE BIKILA

Abebe Bikila of Ethiopia won the marathon at the 1964 Tokyo Olympics. Bikila was presented with a Volkswagen by his appreciative country. In 1969, Bikila was paralyzed in an accident while driving the Volkswagen.

10. FREDERICK LANE

Winners at the 1900 Paris Olympics were given art objects. Frederick Lane of Australia won the 200-meter freestyle swimming competition. Lane was awarded a bronze statue of a horse.

At the 1968 Mexico City Olympics, Tommie Smith and John Carlos stage a protest against the treatment of African-Americans.

Award Ceremonies

Following an Olympic competition, the three medalists are honored at the awards ceremony. While most of the ceremonies are a display of personal and national pride, occasionally something unexpected happens.

1. TOMMIE SMITH AND JOHN CARLOS

American Tommie Smith won the 200-meter run at the 1968 Mexico City Olympics. Teammate John Carlos was the bronze-medal winner. At the awards ceremony, Smith and Carlos decided to use the occasion to protest the treatment of African-Americans. The athletes were barefoot to symbolize poverty. Carlos wore a string of beads that symbolized blacks being unjustly lynched in the past. When the national anthem was played, Smith and Carlos bowed their heads and raised their clenched fists in a Black Power salute. The International Olympic Committee was so outraged by the protest that it expelled Smith and Carlos from the Olympic village and banned them from further competition.

2. VINCE MATTHEWS AND WAYNE COLLETT

Vince Matthews and Wayne Collett finished first and second in the 400-meter run at the 1972 Munich Olympics. Like Tommie Smith and John Carlos, Matthews and Collett were African-Americans. At the awards ceremony, Matthews and Collett did not stand at attention. Instead, they talked and turned away from the flag. Matthews and Collett denied that they were staging a protest, but they were nevertheless banned from Olympic competition.

3. THE 1972 UNITED STATES BASKETBALL TEAM

Members of the United States basketball team were devastated when they lost a controversial 51–50 decision to the Soviet Union in the gold-medal game at the 1972 Munich Olympics. The Americans appeared to have won the game when the Russians were given a second chance to inbound the ball. The winning basket, scored at the buzzer, marked the first time the United States had ever lost an Olympic basketball match. The United States players were so outraged that they refused to accept their silver medals. At the awards ceremony, their place on the podium was empty.

4. GEORGE LYON

Canadian George Lyon won the golf competition at the 1904 St. Louis Olympics. At the awards dinner, Lyon walked on his hands on his way to accept his silver trophy.

5. ANDERS HAUGEN

Anders Haugen finished fourth in the ski-jumping competition at the 1924 Chemonix Winter Olympics. Fifty years later, it was determined that a scoring error had occurred and

Haugen should have finished third. The 83-year-old American was presented with a bronze medal in a ceremony in Oslo.

6. ABEBE BIKILA

Abebe Bikila of Ethiopia won the gold medal in the marathon at the 1964 Tokyo Olympics. Although Bikila was the defending Olympic marathon champion, the Japanese band did not know the Ethiopian national anthem. They played the Japanese national anthem instead.

7. FARID SIMAIKA

Farid Simaika of Egypt was declared the winner of the men's platform diving competition at the 1928 Amsterdam Olympics. After the Egyptian national anthem was played, it was discovered that a scoring error had been made. American Pete Des Jardins was awarded the gold medal and a stunned Simaika accepted the silver medal.

8. ÉTIENNE GAILLY

Étienne Gailly of Belgium was the first man to enter Wembley Stadium in the marathon at the 1948 London Olympics. Totally exhausted, Gailly staggered around the track. On the final lap, he was passed by Delfo Cabrera of Argentina and England's Thomas Richards. Gailly managed to cross the finish line for the bronze medal. He was so exhausted that he was unable to attend the awards ceremony. Rumors circulated that he had died.

9. CHRISTOPHER BRASHER

The 3,000-meter steeplechase at the 1956 Melbourne Olympics ended in controversy. Christopher Brasher of Great

Britain crossed the finish line first but was disqualified for elbowing his way past the second- and third-place finishers, Sándor Rozsnyól of Hungary and Ernst Larsen of Norway. Upon further review, it was decided that Brasher's action did not merit disqualification, and he was declared the winner. Brasher celebrated all night and, in his own words, was "blind drunk" at the awards ceremony. Brasher nearly fell over when the gold medal was placed around his neck.

10. VERNER WECKMAN

Verner Weckman of Finland won the heavyweight Greco-Roman championship at the 1908 London Olympics. Finland was still considered a province of Russia. Instead of raising the Finnish flag at the awards ceremony, a placard with "Finland" written on it was raised in its place.

Multinationals

Nationalism has always been an important part of the Olympics. Athletes represent not only themselves, but their homeland. In some cases, their nationality was not clear-cut.

1. NAIM SÜLEYMANOGLU

Naim Süleymanoglu was born in Bulgaria. The weightlifter competed for Bulgaria until 1986, when he defected to Turkey. Süleymanoglu, born of Turkish ancestry, wanted to compete for Turkey at the 1988 Seoul Olympics. According to the Olympic rules, an athlete had to wait three years before representing another country unless he received a waiver from the country in which he had lived. The Turkish government paid Bulgaria more than a million dollars for permission to let Süleymanoglu compete for Turkey. The move paid off when he won a gold medal in the featherweight division of the weightlifting competition at Seoul. He also won gold medals in the featherweight division at the 1992 and 1996 Olympics.

2. **MICHEL THÉATO**

Michel Théato won the gold medal in the men's marathon at the 1900 Paris Olympics. For years it was believed that he was from France. An Olympic scholar eventually discovered that Théato was actually from Luxembourg.

3. **1996 CANADIAN 4×100-METER RELAY**

The Canadian men's 4×100-meter relay team upset the United States to win the gold medal at the 1996 Atlanta Olympics. What made the team unique was that none of its members were born in Canada. Donovan Bailey and Robert Esmie were born in Jamaica, Bruny Surin was born in Haiti, and Glenray Gilbert was from Trinidad.

4. **LUDMILA ENGQUIST**

Ludmila Narozhilenko competed for the Soviet Union in the 100-meter hurdles at the 1988 and 1992 Olympics. She did not reach the finals in either Games. She married a Swede, Johan Engquist, and was granted Swedish citizenship prior to the 1996 Atlanta Olympics. Competing for Sweden, Ludmila Engquist won the gold medal in the 100-meter hurdles at the 1996 Games.

5. **FIONA MAY**

Fiona May finished sixth in the women's long jump while competing for Great Britain at the 1988 Seoul Olympics. May later married an Italian and won a silver medal in the long jump while representing Italy at the 1996 Atlanta Olympics.

6. **MARC GIRARDELLI**

An Austrian citizen who competed for Luxembourg, skier Marc Girardelli was not permitted to participate in the 1980 and 1984 Winter Olympics. The ban was lifted for the 1988 Calgary Winter Games, but Girardelli did not win a medal. Finally, in 1992, Girardelli went home from Albertville with two silvers.

7. ZOLA BUDD

South Africa was banned from the Olympics in 1960 because of its policy of apartheid. One of the athletes punished by the ban was middle-distance runner Zola Budd. It appeared that the teenage sensation would be unable to compete in the 1984 Los Angeles Olympics. Because Budd's grandfather had been a British citizen, she was awarded British citizenship and was allowed to compete. In the 3,000 meters, Budd was leading when American Mary Decker stepped on her heel and fell heavily. Budd eventually faded to finish seventh.

8. WALTER WINANS

Walter Winans's parents were living in Russia when he was born. Winans, a world-class marksman, spent most of his life living in England. He competed for the United States in the 1908 London Olympics and won a gold medal in the running-deer-shooting double-shot event. He was permitted to represent the United States only on the condition that he swear allegiance and return to America and resume his citizenship.

9. NORMAN PRITCHARD

Norman Pritchard finished second in the 200-meter dash at the 1900 Paris Olympics. Originally, it was thought that Pritchard represented India, but just prior to the Olympics, he declared his intention to compete for Great Britain.

10. **PETER O'CONNOR**

Peter O'Connor won the gold medal in the triple jump at the 1906 Athens Olympics. Technically the Irishman competed for Great Britain since Ireland had not yet won its independence. When the British flag, the Union Jack, was hoisted, O'Connor climbed the flagpole and unfurled an Irish flag.

Rules Are Meant to Be Broken

The Olympics are supposed to represent the pinnacle of sportsmanship. There have been times, however, when competitors stretched the rules to gain that extra edge.

1. STELLA WALSH

Stella Walsh was one of the greatest runners of her time. The highlight of her celebrated career was a gold medal in the women's 100-meter dash at the 1932 Los Angeles Olympics. On December 4, 1980, Walsh was shot to death during a robbery attempt in Cleveland. During the autopsy it was revealed that Walsh had actually been a man.

2. FRED LORZ

American Fred Lorz was the first competitor to cross the finish line in the men's marathon at the 1904 St. Louis Olympics. He was about to be declared the winner when it was discovered that he had ridden in an automobile for 11 of the 26 miles. Lorz was disqualified and another American, Thomas Hicks, was declared the champion.

3. **SPIRIDON BELOKAS**

It appeared that Greek runners had swept the top three places in the men's marathon at the 1896 Athens Olympics. The third-place finisher was Spiridon Belokas. The initial joy turned to shame when word came that Belokas had ridden part of the way in a carriage. He was publicly humiliated and stripped of his shirt. Belokas was disqualified and a Hungarian runner, Gyula Kellner, was moved up to third place.

4. **BORIS ONISCHENCKO**

One of the most outrageous examples of cheating occurred in the pentathlon competition at the 1976 Montreal Olympics. In the fencing portion of the competition, Boris Onischencko of the Soviet Union used a rigged épée. The wired sword registered a hit when he pushed a concealed button. His plan was foiled and Onischencko and his Soviet team were disqualified.

5. **FRANK SHORTER**

A cruel hoax deprived Frank Shorter of his moment of glory at the end of the men's marathon at the 1972 Munich Olympics. Norbert Sudhaus, a German college student, ran into the stadium. Most of the crowd, awaiting the marathon leader, assumed he was the leader and began to cheer. Sudhaus ran a full lap before security caught up with him. As he was led off the track, the real leader, American Frank Shorter, entered the stadium. The crowd began to boo and whistle at the impostor. Shorter, bewildered, could not understand why he was getting a negative reaction. Only later did he learn the truth.

American Frank Shorter held on to his lead to win gold in the marathon at the 1972 Munich Olympics.

6. CARROLL BURTON

American lightweight boxer Carroll Burton won his first-round match at the 1904 St. Louis Olympics. The boxer was really an impostor named Bollinger. When his true identity was revealed, Bollinger was disqualified.

7. MARGARET DE JESUS

Madeline de Jesus was a member of the 1984 Puerto Rican 4×400-meter relay team. Madeline was injured while competing in the long jump. Her twin sister, Margaret, took her place in a qualifiying heat of the 4×400-meter relay. After the Puerto Rican coach discovered the switch, he withdrew his team from the competition.

8. DAINIS KŪLA

Dainis Kūla of the Soviet Union won the gold medal in the javelin throw at the 1980 Moscow Olympics. The victory was somewhat tarnished when it was charged that officials had been opening the doors at the end of the stadium when the Soviet athletes threw the javelin. It was thought that the added tailwind increased the distance of their throws.

9. MICHEL THÉATO

The 1900 Olympic marathon was run through the streets of Paris. Michel Théato of Luxembourg was the only runner to finish the race in less than three hours. Suspicious American runners accused him of taking shortcuts, but the charges were never proven.

10. CARABINIER AND MAMIE

The regatta open-class yachting competition at the 1900 Paris Olympics was a debacle. With virtually no wind, only 7 of the 49 yachts finished the race. Two of the boats that completed the course, Carabinier and Mamie, were disqualified for using motorized propulsion instead of sails.

Olympic Controversies

Every Olympics has had its share of controversies. Here are some of the most controversial moments in Olympic history.

1. JOHN DEVITT

The outcome of the 100-meter freestyle swimming competition at the 1960 Rome Olympics is still being debated today. It appeared that American Lance Larson touched the wall just ahead of Australian John Devitt. The electronic timer registered a time of 55.1 seconds for Larson and 55.2 for Devitt. Devitt, believing that Larson had won, congratulated the American after the race. At the time the official decision was made by a panel of judges. However, the head judge, Hans Runstromer, declared Devitt the winner. In order to make the official time agree with the decision, Larson's time was changed to 55.2 seconds.

2. WYNDHAM HALSWELLE

The 400-meter run at the 1908 London Olympics matched Wyndham Halswelle of Great Britain against three

Americans: William Robbins, John Taylor, and John Carpenter. The race for the gold medal appeared to be between Halswelle and Carpenter. The American crossed the finish line first in 48.4 seconds, but British officials immediately claimed that he had intentionally blocked Halswelle's path. They disqualified Carpenter and ordered the race rerun. The other Americans refused to run, and Hallswelle ran alone to win the gold medal in a walkover.

3. IRINA AND TAMARA PRESS

Tamara and Irina Press of the Soviet Union won a combined five gold medals. Tamara won the shot-put competitions at the 1960 Rome and 1964 Tokyo Olympics and the discus throw at the 1964 Games. Irina, her younger sister, won the 80-meter hurdles at the 1964 Tokyo Olympics. The Press sisters were so powerful that some observers questioned their sexuality. Curiously, when sex tests were instituted, the Press sisters retired from track and field competition.

4. ZOLTÁN HALMAJ

One of the closest finishes in Olympic history occurred at the 50-yard freestyle swimming competition at the 1904 St. Louis Olympics. American Scott Leary and Hungarian Zoltán Halmaj matched each other stroke for stroke. Ten feet from the finish, the Hungarian judge yelled that Halmaj was the winner. At the finish, it appeared that the Hungarian may have touched first. However, the American judge declared that, in his opinion, Leary had won. A near-brawl broke out between the two sides. When the matter could not be resolved, it was decided that the race had to be rerun. This time Halmaj won easily.

5. **ERIC GRIFFIN**

Olympic boxing has had its share of questionable decisions. A new computerized system was installed at the 1992 Barcelona Olympics in the hopes of eliminating unfair decisions. Judges were instructed to push a button when a fighter landed a scoring punch. Unfortunately, the judges had trouble at first with the new system. In a light flyweight bout between Eric Griffin of the United States and Spain's Rafael Lozano, the Spaniard won the decision 6–5 even though all five judges had Griffin ahead on their cards.

6. **ALEKSANDR PORTNOV**

At the 1980 Moscow Olympics, the swimming and diving competitions were sometimes held simultaneously. Soviet platform diver Aleksandr Portnov claimed he badly missed his backward two-and-a-half somersault dive because he was distracted by the sounds of the crowd shouting during the 100-meter butterfly swimming race, held in an adjacent pool. The diver protested to officials, but Portnov's complaint was ignored. The poor dive dropped Portnov from medal contention. Three other divers also protested to no avail.

7. **JEAN SHILEY**

Americans Jean Shiley and Babe Didrikson both set Olympic records with leaps of 5 feet, 5 ¼ inches in the high-jump competition at the 1932 Los Angeles Olympics. In a jump-off, both women again cleared the same height. The judge announced that Shiley was the winner because Didrikson was using an illegal technique. The western roll style Didrikson used allowed her to dive over the bar. According to the rules at the time, a jumper's head was not allowed to clear the bar before her body. Rather than disqualify her, the judges awarded Didrikson the silver medal. The western roll technique was made legal soon thereafter and became the standard for high jumpers.

8. DAN HORTON

The pole vault at the 1900 Paris Olympics was scheduled to be held on Sunday, July 15. Two of the favorites, Dan Horton and Bascom Johnson, did not vault because they refused to compete on the Sabbath. They were reassured that the competition would continue on Monday. Officials changed their minds and declared the Sunday results final. Subsequently, two unofficial pole-vault competitions were held. Bascom Johnson won the first and Dan Horton the second. Both men cleared heights above the winning vault of gold medalist Irving Baxter.

9. BOB SEAGREN

Bob Seagren of the United States won the gold medal in the pole vault at the 1968 Mexico City Olympics. The world record holder was also favored to win the gold at the 1972 Munich Summer Games. Before the competition, officials announced a ban on the brand of pole Seagren and some of the other contenders were using because the brand had not been available to all vaulters for a year. Forced to use a borrowed pole, Seagren finished second behind East German Wolfgang Nordwig.

10. RALPH ROSE

One of the most controversial moments at the Olympics took place at the opening ceremonies of the 1908 London Games. As the athletes from different nations paraded past

Bob Seagren pole-vaults his way to gold at the 1968 Mexico City Games.

King Edward VII, the flagbearers dipped their flags in his honor. But Ralph Rose, the 1904 shot put gold medalist, did not dip the American flag. Martin Sheridan, an American who won the gold medal in the shot put at the 1906 Athens Olympics, said, "The flag dips for no earthly king." It began a tradition that continues to this day.

Official Business

Olympic officials can sometimes affect the outcome of events.

1. ORESTE PULITI

Italian fencer Oreste Puliti was one of the favorites to win the gold medal in the individual sabre competition at the 1924 Paris Olympics. When he easily defeated three of his Italian teammates, a Hungarian judge, György Kovács, accused the Italians of losing on purpose to conserve Puliti's strength for later matches. Puliti was disqualified, and a Hungarian fencer, Sandor Posta, won the gold medal. A few days later, Puliti punched Kovács in the nose and challenged him to a duel. Four months later, the men met in a duel. Although both were wounded, the injuries were not serious. With their honor restored, they shook hands and left the field of battle.

2. ACHILLE PICCINI

A soccer match between the United States and Italy at the 1936 Berlin Olympics got out of control. A German referee named Weingärtner threw Italian Achille Piccini out of the game because of his rough play. Piccini not only refused to leave the field, but some of his teammates attempted to intimidate the referee. They grabbed Weingärtner and put their hands over his mouth. Italy won the game 1–0.

3. JOSEPH MCCLUSKEY

Chaos reigned because of an error by an official in the 3,000-meter steeplechase at the 1932 Los Angeles Olympics. The official lost count of the laps, and as a result, the athletes ran one lap too many. American Joseph McCluskey, who would have won the silver medal at the correct distance, was passed on the extra lap and finished third.

4. EMIL ZÁTOPEK

Another lap-counting mistake occurred in the men's 10,000-meter run at the 1948 London Olympics. An official signaled to the runners that they were on the final lap when they still had one lap to go. Czech runner Emil Zátopek won by nearly 50 seconds and was not affected by the blunder, but the confusion may have affected the other placings.

5. HARRY VENN

Harry Venn was a judge in walking competitions at the 1908 London Olympics. For some unknown reason, Venn wandered into the path of Belgian cyclist Guillaume Coeckelberg during a qualifying heat of the 100-kilometer cycling competition. Coeckelberg suffered cuts in the fall but managed to finish the race and qualify for the final. Still feeling the effects of his injuries, Coeckelberg did not complete the 100-kilometer race.

6. **EDWARD GLOVER**

Edward Glover won the bronze medal in the pole vault at the 1906 Athens Olympics, but he might have done better were it not for the mindless act of an official. As Glover was about to attempt a vault, he collided with an official. Glover was injured and could not improve on his best previous vault.

7. **BOB MATHIAS**

An absent-minded official nearly cost Bob Mathias the gold medal in the decathlon at the 1948 London Olympics. The discus was Mathias's best decathlon event, and it was essential that he make a good throw if he hoped to win the gold medal. Mathias made a great throw, but an official accidentally picked up the marker where the discus landed. Officials spent a half hour trying to determine the distance. Finally, he was credited with a throw of 144 feet, 4 inches. The distance was probably not as long as Mathias's throw, but it was good enough for him to win a gold medal.

8. **MAURICE SCHILLES**

At the 1908 London Olympics, the 1,000-meter match sprint cycling race was declared a non-event because the winning time was too slow. A time limit of 1 minute and 45 seconds had been put on the race to keep cyclists from endlessly jockeying for position. Maurice Schilles of France finished first but did not beat the time limit. Most of the cyclists assumed the judges would permit a rerun, but instead they declared the race void and no medals were awarded.

9. **1968 BOXING JUDGES**

Boxing judges at the Olympics are almost always controversial, but never more so than at the 1968 Mexico City

Bob Mathias won the decathlon in the 1948 and 1952 Olympics. Here he throws the discus, his best event, at the 1948 London Games.

Olympics. More than a dozen judges and referees were dismissed for incompetence.

10. **LUIS FOURNIER**

The officiating at the 1980 Moscow Olympics left much to be desired. There were numerous instances of officiating that favored Soviet athletes. In the men's discus, Viktor Raschupkin of the Soviet Union won the gold medal. Many observers felt that Luis Fournier of Cuba may have been cheated out of the gold. It appeared that he was not credited with the proper distance on his throws. In particular, his final throw appeared to be worthy of the gold medal. Fournier had to be satisfied with a bronze medal instead.

Prolonged Protests

Protests at the Olympics have come in many forms.

1. BYUN JONG-IL

At the 1988 Seoul Olympics, Korean bantamweight boxer Byun Jong-il set a record for a sit-down protest. He lost a close decision to Alexander Hristov of Bulgaria because he had been penalized two points for head butts. Jong-il protested the decision by sitting in the ring for one hour and seven minutes.

2. CHOH DONG-KIH

The previous record for a sit-down protest in an Olympic match was set by South Korean flyweight Choh Dong-kih at the 1964 Tokyo Summer Games. Dong-kih was disqualified for holding his head too low in a match against Stanislav Sorokin of the Soviet Union. In protest, Dong-kih sat down in the middle of the ring for 51 minutes.

3. GEORGE SHELDON

American George Sheldon won the platform diving competition at the 1904 St. Louis Olympics. German Georg Hoffmann finished second. The Germans filed a protest because they believed Hoffmann's dives were more difficult than Sheldon's. They believed the quality of the entries did not matter. While Sheldon's dives emphasized clean entries, the German divers frequently did belly flops. The protest was disallowed a week later.

4. THE 1900 AMERICAN TUG-OF-WAR TEAM

Incredibly, the tug-of-war was a medal event in six Olympics. Footwear was a constant source of controversy. The American team at the 1900 Paris Olympics wanted to compete in spiked shoes, but other teams protested that such shoes gave them an unfair advantage. The Americans decided to tug barefoot. They were unable to compete in the final because three members of their team were taking part in the hammer throw.

5. DICK GRANT

American Dick Grant finished sixth in the men's marathon at the 1900 Paris Olympics. He argued that just as he was about to pass eventual winner Michel Théato, he was knocked down by a mysterious cyclist on the streets of Paris. Grant not only filed a protest, he filed a lawsuit contending that the collision had been intentional. Grant lost both the protest and the lawsuit.

6. NIKOLAI PANIN

Controversy with figure skating judging is nothing new. At the 1900 Paris Olympics, Russian skater Nikolai Panin withdrew in protest after the compulsory-figures section of the competition. Panin blamed biased judging for his second-place showing behind eventual champion Ulrich Salchow of Sweden.

7. IRISH REPUBLICAN ARMY

Four members of the Irish Republican Army made a surprise appearance in the road-race cycling competition at the 1972 Munich Olympics. They were protesting the Irish Cycling Federation because they had competed against cyclists from Northern Ireland. The only incident came when one of the IRA members tried to run Irish cyclist Noël Taggart off the road. Taggart did not win a medal, and the four uninvited cyclists were arrested.

8. 1948 UNITED STATES 4×100-METER RELAY TEAM

The United States men's 4×100-meter relay team at the 1948 London Olympics finished half a second ahead of the British team. The Americans' gold-medal performance was put in jeopardy when a judge determined that the pass on the first leg from Barney Ewell to Lorenzo Wright had taken place beyond the legal passing lane. The United States team was disqualified, and the British were awarded the gold medal. The United States filed a protest. Days later, the disqualification was overturned, and they were presented with their gold medals.

9. 1904 4×50-YARD FREESTYLE SWIMMING

The 4×50-yard men's freestyle swimming competition featured teams from individual swimming clubs. The United States protested when the Germans entered a team that consisted of athletes from four different swimming clubs. The protest was upheld, and the German team was disqualified. A team from The New York Athletic Club won the competition.

10. **KHALID SKAH**

The men's 10,000-meter run was one of the most controversial events at the 1992 Barcelona Olympics. The winner was Khalid Skah of Morocco. During the race, another Moroccan runner, Hammou Boutayeb, appeared to intentionally interfere with Skah's closest competition. The interference was so blatant that an official actually attempted to pull Boutayeb off the track. Skah was disqualified, and second-place finisher Richard Chelimo of Kenya was declared the winner. Skah immediately protested, claiming that there had been no collusion between himself and Boutayeb. The jury of appeal decided that the interference was not serious enough to merit a disqualification and awarded the gold medal to Skah.

Disqualified!

Olympic athletes have been disqualified for nearly every reason imaginable. American George Guthrie finished third in the 110-meter hurdles competition at the 1924 Paris Olympics but was disqualified for knocking over three hurdles, an infraction of the rules at the time. Puerto Rican flyweight boxer Heriberto Cintron was disqualified at the 1968 Mexico City Olympics for being a year younger than the age limit of 17.

1. JIM THORPE

Jim Thorpe won gold medals in the decathlon and pentathlon at the 1912 Stockholm Olympics. Six months later, Thorpe was stripped of his gold medals because it was revealed that he had earned $60 a month playing semi-pro baseball in North Carolina in 1908. He had also briefly played minor league baseball, earning a salary of $25 per week. The strict amateur guidelines stated that an Olympic athlete could not have been paid for participating in any sport. The medals were returned to the Thorpe family in 1983, but Jim Thorpe never lived to see it. The man voted

Basketball player, football player, and Olympic athlete, Jim Thorpe was one of the greatest athletes of the twentieth century.

the greatest athlete of the first half of the twentieth century had died in 1953.

2. **EVANDER HOLYFIELD**

Evander Holyfield fought Kevin Barry of New Zealand in the semifinals of the light heavyweight boxing competition at the 1984 Los Angeles Olympics. At the end of the second round, Holyfield floored Barry with a left hook. Referee Gligorije Novicic of Yugoslavia counted out Barry and then shocked the crowd by disqualifying Holyfield for hitting the New Zealander after he had called for them to break. Holyfield, a future heavyweight boxing champion, was awarded the bronze instead of having an opportunity to fight for the gold. Even the winner, Barry, was denied a chance to fight for the gold medal. A rule stated that no amateur boxer could fight again until four weeks after he had been knocked out. Barry was given the silver medal.

3. **GEHNÄLL PERSSON**

Sweden won the gold medal in the team dressage equestrian competition at the 1948 London Olympics. The team was disqualified eight months later because one of its members, Gehnäll Persson, was not an officer as he had claimed. Only commissioned officers were permitted to compete at the time. France was belatedly awarded the gold medal.

4. **1988 CANADIAN SKI TEAM**

The Canadian men's ski team was disqualified prior to the giant slalom competition at the 1988 Calgary Winter Olympics because of what they wore. It was determined that their ski suits had not been submitted for a safety inspection.

5. HANK LAMMENS

Forgetfulness resulted in Hank Lammens being disqualified from the Finn-class sailing competition at the 1992 Barcelona Olympics. The world-class yachtsman was disqualified for forgetting to bring his life jacket.

6. ALI KAZEMI

Iranian boxer Ali Kazemi forgot something important during the light heavyweight competition at the 1992 Barcelona Games. Kazemi was disqualified for not bringing his boxing gloves.

7. BERTIL SANDSTRØM

In the individual dressage equestrian competition at the 1932 Los Angeles Olympics, Bertil Sandstrøm of Sweden was disqualified for making clicking sounds to motivate his horse.

8. CARLO AIROLDI

Carlo Airoldi of Italy wanted to compete in the 1896 Olympics so badly that he walked from his hometown of Milan to Athens, Greece. One of the reasons for the thousand-mile walk was to get in shape for the men's marathon. When he arrived, he found that he was disqualified from the event because he had previously received prize money for running and was considered a professional.

9. ORTRUN ENDERLEIN AND ANNA-MARIA MÜLLER

Ortrun Enderlein and Anna-Maria Müller of the German Democratic Republic finished first and second in the women's luge competition at the 1968 Grenoble Winter

Olympics. Enderlein had also won the luge competition at the 1964 Innsbruck Games. Both Enderlein and Müller were disqualified when it was discovered that the runners of their sleds had been heated to increase their speed down the course. The Germans denied the charges and blamed them on a "capitalist plot." Müller came back to win the gold medal in the luge at the 1972 Sapporo Winter Olympics.

10. **JOE LAZARUS**

American boxer Joe Lazarus knocked out Swedish opponent Oscar Andren in a bantamweight bout in the 1924 Paris Olympics. Lazarus was promptly disqualified by referee Maurice Siegel for hitting during a break. Siegel later admitted that he had made a mistake, and Andren graciously offered a rematch, but Olympic officials would not permit it.

Drug Busts

More than 50 athletes have been disqualified for testing positive for drugs at the Olympics. The performance-enhancing substances have ranged from caffeine to anabolic steroids.

1. BEN JOHNSON

Ben Johnson of Canada set a world record when he was clocked in 9.79 seconds in winning the 100-meter dash at the 1988 Seoul Olympics. When Johnson was tested for drugs, traces of stanozolol, an anabolic steroid, were found in his system. Johnson was stripped of his gold medal and world record. His biggest rival, American Carl Lewis, was awarded the gold medal.

2. RICK DEMONT

One of the most unfortunate drug disqualifications happened to American swimmer Rick DeMont. He won the 400-meter freestyle competition at the 1972 Munich Olympics. DeMont was disqualified when the banned drug ephedrine was found in his system. DeMont had taken an asthma medication, unaware that it contained the illegal substance.

3. ANDREA RADUCAN

Andrea Raducan became the first Romanian woman gymnast to win the all-around Olympic competition since Nadia Comaneci when she finished first at the 2000 Sydney Olympics. Her joy was short-lived because she was stripped of the all-around gold medal when she tested positive for the drug pseudoephedrine. She had unwittingly taken a cold medication that contained the banned substance. Her teammate Simona Amanar was awarded the gold medal.

4. KORNELIA ENDER

Kornelia Ender won four gold medals in swimming events at the 1976 Summer Olympics. More than a decade after she dominated the women's swimming competition in Montreal, it was revealed that Ender and many other East German athletes had been administered anabolic steroids without their knowledge.

5. KRISTIN OTTO

Another East German swimmer who was given prohibited drugs to enhance her performance was Kristin Otto. She won six gold medals at the 1988 Seoul Olympics.

6. HANS-GUNNAR LILJENWALL

The dubious distinction of being the first Olympic athlete to be disqualified for testing positive for a banned substance was Hans-Gunnar Liljenwall of Sweden. He was disqualified from the pentathlon at the 1968 Mexico City Olympics.

Liljenwell tested positive for alcohol. He had drunk two beers to calm his nerves before the shooting competition.

7. PAUL CERUTTI

Sixty-five-year-old Paul Cerutti of Monaco was disqualified from the trap-shooting competition at the 1976 Montreal Olympics. He tested positive for amphetamines.

8. BAKAAVAA BUIDAA

Bakaavaa Buidaa of Mongolia won the silver medal in the lightweight judo competition at the 1972 Munich Olympics. Buidaa was disqualified for failing a drug test. It was determined that he had too much caffeine in his system.

9. VALENTIN HRISTOV

Not surprisingly, strength-enhancing drugs frequently turn up in the systems of weightlifters. Valentin Hristov of Bulgaria was stripped of his gold medal in the heavyweight division of the 1976 Montreal Olympics when he tested positive for steroids.

10. GALINA KULAKOVA

Galina Kulakova of the Soviet Union was the gold medalist in the five-kilometer Nordic skiing competition at the 1972 Sapporo Olympics. She finished third in the five-kilometer race at the 1976 Innsbruck Olympics but was disqualified for testing positive for the drug ephedrine. She had inhaled nasal spray that contained the banned drug.

Resorting to Violence

One of the Olympic ideals is to bring athletes from around the world together in peaceful competition. Unfortunately, violence has frequently reared its ugly head at the Olympics.

1. VALENTIN LOREN

Spanish featherweight Valentin Loren was disqualified for holding in a bout at the 1964 Tokyo Olympics. Incensed, he punched referee György Sermer in the face. Loren was banned from amateur boxing for life.

2. EDWIN FLACK

Australian Edwin Flack led the men's marathon at the 1896 Athens Olympics with two miles to go when he began to stagger. A good Samaritan along the road reached out to keep him from falling. Flack, who mistakenly believed he was being attacked, beat the man to the ground. The exhausted and nearly delirious runner dropped out of the race.

3. 1956 HUNGARIAN WATER POLO TEAM

In November 1956, Soviet troops invaded Hungary to crush an uprising. A month later, Hungary and the Soviet Union met in a water polo match at the 1956 Melbourne Olympics. There was literally blood in the water. Hungarian player Ervin Zádor left the pool with a huge gash over his left eye, the result of a head butt from Russian Valentin Prokopov. Angered Hungarian spectators jumped into the pool, and the match was called. Hungary was credited with a 4–0 victory.

4. 1952 URUGUAYAN BASKETBALL TEAM

The Uruguayans turned basketball into basketbrawl at the 1952 Helsinki Olympics. In a game against France, all but three of the Uruguayan players fouled out. When Uruguay lost the game, Uruguayan players and fans attacked referee Vincent Farrell. Two players were banned from the competition. The Uruguayans were not through. Three Soviet players were injured in a subsequent game against Uruguay. The bronze-medal game between Uruguay and Argentina was marred by a near-riot involving players and fans. Uruguay won the game by the score of 60–59.

5. LEE HEUNG-SOO

Korean bantamweight boxer Byun Jong-li lost a decision at the 1988 Seoul Olympics after he was penalized two points for head butts. Korean boxing trainer Lee Heung-soo punched referee Keith Walker, inciting a riot. The ring filled with Koreans who attacked Walker mercilessly. Walker escaped serious injury and immediately left Seoul.

6. **MARK SCHULTZ**

Turkish freestyle wrestler Resit Karabacek suffered a broken left elbow in a middleweight match against American Mark Schultz at the 1984 Los Angeles Olympics. The Turkish wrestling team filed a protest that Schultz had used an illegal hold. Strangely, while the protest was upheld and Karabacek was declared the winner, Schultz was not excluded from the tournament. In fact, Schultz went on to win the gold medal.

7. **ARRACHION**

Wrestling matches at the ancient Greek Olympics were frequently violent. Arrachion was caught in a choke hold when he broke his opponent's toe, causing him to submit. Arrachion died from the choke hold but was declared Olympic champion posthumously.

8. **1932 BRAZIL WATER POLO TEAM**

The Brazil water polo team did not exhibit good sportsmanship in a game against Germany at the 1932 Los Angeles Olympics. Following a 7–3 loss, the team attacked referee Béla Komjadi and chased him into the stands. The Brazilians were barred from competition for the remainder of the games.

9. **KARL ÖBERG**

Swedish player Karl Öberg hit Canadian coach David Bauer over the head with his stick during a 3–1 loss in the hockey competition at the 1964 Innsbruck Winter Olympics. Despite the loss, Sweden won the silver medal, while Canada did not medal.

10. **MARJUT LUKKARINEN**

Marjut Lukkarinen of Finland won the gold medal in the five-kilometer Nordic skiing competition at the 1992 Albertville Winter Olympics. During the race, she encountered a slower skier, Katerina Neumannová of Czechoslovakia. When Neumannová did not respond to her cries to move over and let her pass, Lukkarinen began striking her on the legs with her ski poles.

Death at the Olympics

Athletes and spectators have been killed at the Olympic Games.

1. 1964 PERU-ARGENTINA SOCCER MATCH

On May 24, 1964, Argentina met Peru in an Olympic soccer qualifying match held in Lima, Peru. Argentina led Peru 1–0 with two minutes remaining in the game. It appeared that Peru had tied the game, but the referee nullified the goal. Angry fans poured onto the field and a riot ensued. The stadium was set on fire, and, by the time order was restored, 328 people were dead, most of them crushed by the crowd.

2. PALESTINIAN TERRORISTS

One of the darkest moments in Olympic history occurred at the 1972 Munich Summer Games. Palestinian terrorist group Black September occupied the Israeli team headquarters in the Olympic village. An athlete and coach were murdered. The terrorists demanded the release of more than 200 Arab prisoners held in Israel and other countries. During a shootout at the airport, the terrorists killed all nine Israeli hostages. Five terrorists and one police officer were also killed during the shoot-out.

3. ATLANTA BOMBING

One person was killed and more than 100 were injured when a bomb exploded at Centennial Olympic Park during the 1996 Atlanta Olympics. Although authorities believe they know who was responsible for the bombing, the suspect has never been apprehended.

4. FRANCISCO LAZARO

Portuguese runner Francisco Lazaro collapsed at the 19-mile mark of the marathon at the 1912 Stockholm Olympics. Suffering from heatstroke, Lazaro died the next day.

5. KNUD JENSEN

Near the end of the time-trial cycling competition at the 1960 Rome Olympics, Danish cyclist Knud Jensen fell off his bicycle. The temperature was above 90 degrees, and it was assumed Jensen had suffered a heatstroke. Jensen fractured his skull and died a few hours later. It was revealed that Jensen had taken drugs to stimulate circulation prior to the race, and they may have contributed to his death.

6. ROSS MILNE

Ross Milne, a 19-year-old Australian skier, was killed during a practice run for the men's downhill at the 1964 Innsbruck Winter Olympics. He struck a tree while traveling at 60 miles per hour and died instantly.

7. KAZIMIERZ KAY-SKRZYPESKI

The inaugural luge competition at the 1964 Innsbruck Winter Olympics was marred by the death of Kazimierz Kay-Skrzypeski. The Polish athlete was killed during a crash on a practice run.

8. 1906 ATHENS OLYMPICS

During the 1906 Athens Olympics, government troops violently disbursed a political demonstration. Three people were killed.

9. KONICHI TSUBURAYA

Konichi Tsuburaya of Japan won a bronze medal in the men's marathon at the 1964 Tokyo Olympics. Tsuburaya set his sights on winning the gold medal at the 1968 Mexico City Olympics. Slowed by injuries, he committed suicide by cutting his throat with a razor blade in January 1968.

10. JURG OBERHAMMER

A freak accident took the life of Austrian surgeon Jurg Oberhammer during the 1988 Calgary Olympics. He collided with another skier on the slopes and was killed when he fell beneath a snow plow.

Killed in Action

The Olympics bring together athletes from nations around the world in peaceful competition. Unfortunately, wars between nations cancelled the 1916, 1940, and 1944 Olympics. Many Olympic athletes gave their lives fighting for their countries.

1. BILLY FISKE

Billy Fiske won gold medals in the four-man bobsled competitions at the 1928 and 1932 Winter Olympics. Fiske, an American, married a British countess and moved to England. When war broke out in Europe, Fiske joined the Royal Air Force. On August 16, 1940, Fiske was killed in action, the first American-born pilot to die in World War II. Fiske was only 29 years old.

2. WYNDHAM HALSWELLE

Wyndham Halswelle of Great Britain was the gold medalist in the 400-meter run at the 1908 London Olympics.

Halswelle was killed on March 31, 1915, while fighting in France during World War I.

3. TAKEICHI NISHI

Takeichi Nishi of Japan won the individual jumping equestrian competition at the 1932 Los Angeles Olympics. A colonel in the Japanese army, Nishi committed suicide rather than surrender during the Battle of Iwo Jima.

4. LUZ LONG

German Luz Long finished second behind Jesse Owens in the long jump at the 1936 Berlin Olympics. Long was killed during the Battle of San Pietro in Italy on July 14, 1943.

5. JEAN BOUIN AND GEORGE HUTSON

Jean Bouin of France and George Hutson of Great Britain finished second and third in the 5,000-meter run at the 1912 Stockholm Olympics. Both Bouin and Hutson were killed in action in September 1914.

6. JANUSZ KUSOCIÑSKI

Janusz Kusociñski won the gold medal in the 10,000-meter run at the 1932 Los Angeles Olympics. When Germany invaded Poland, Kusociñski joined the restistance movement. Arrested by the Nazis, he was executed on June 21, 1940.

7. CLIFF CUSHMAN

The silver medalist in the 400-meter hurdles at the 1960 Rome Olympics, American Cliff Cushman was killed in Vietnam in 1966.

8. LEWIS CLIVE

Lewis Clive won a gold medal in the pair-oared-shell-without-coxswain rowing competition at the 1932 Los Angeles Olympics. The Englishman was killed in fighting during the Spanish Civil War in 1938.

9. ALFRED FLATOW

German gymnast Alfred Flatow, winner of the gold medal in the parallel bars at the 1896 Athens Olympics, earned three gold medals and one silver for Germany. The Olympic hero died in a Nazi concentration camp in 1945.

10. RUDOLF HARBIG

A bronze medalist in the men's 4×400-meter relay team at the 1936 Berlin Olympics, German Rudolf Harbig was killed fighting on the Russian front in March 1944.

Unusual Deaths

S ome Olympic athletes met with bizarre deaths.

1. LARRY ANDREASEN

Larry Andreasen won the bronze medal in men's springboard diving at the 1964 Tokyo Olympics. Years later, Andreasen became obsessed with setting the record for diving from the highest bridge. After several successful jumps, Andreasen was killed in 1990 when he tried jumping from the Vincent Thomas Bridge in Los Angeles.

2. YELENA MIROSHINA

Yelena Miroshina won the silver medal in platform diving at the 1992 Barcelona Olympics. Three years later, the 21-year-old committed suicide by jumping from a ninth story window in Moscow.

3. BRUCE HARLAN

At the 1948 London Olympics, Bruce Harlan of the United States won a gold medal in springboard diving and a silver in platform diving. In 1959, Harlan was killed when he fell from a diving tower following a diving exhibition in Connecticut.

4. ROD MILBURN

Rod Milburn was one of the greatest hurdlers in United States track and field history. He won the gold medal in the 110-meter hurdles at the 1972 Munich Olympics. In 1997, Milburn died in an accident while working in a paper plant in Louisiana. Milburn fell into a hopper car filled with crystallized sodium chlorate and scalding water.

5. CHUNG SE-HOON

The bronze medalist in lightweight judo at the 1992 Barcelona Olympics, Korean Chung Se-hoon hoped to compete in the 1996 Atlanta Olympics in the half-lightweight division. Four months before the Olympics, he died of a heart attack after going on a crash diet to lose the necessary weight.

6. DAVID SCHULTZ

David Schultz dominated the opposition to win the gold medal in the welterweight freestyle wrestling competition at the 1984 Los Angeles Olympics. On January 26, 1996, Schultz was inexplicably murdered by millionaire John du Pont, a patron of the United States wrestling team.

7. ELIAS KATZ

Elias Katz of Finland won a silver medal in the 3,000-meter steeplechase at the 1924 Paris Olympics. Twenty-three years later, he was murdered by Arab terrorists while living in Gaza.

8. ED SANDERS

American heavyweight boxer Ed Sanders defeated future heavyweight champion Ingemar Johansson to win the gold medal at the 1952 Helsinki Olympics. Sanders died from brain injuries following a professional boxing match in December 1954.

9. FABIO CASARTELLI

Fabio Casartelli of Italy won the gold medal in the road-race cycling competition at the 1992 Barcelona Olympics. Casartelli was competing in the 1995 Tour de France when he was killed in a fall while cycling in the Pyrenees Mountains.

10. FÉLIX ENDRICH

Félix Endrich and Friedrich Waller of Switzerland won the two-man bobsled competition at the 1948 St. Moritz Winter Olympics. Endrich died in 1953 when his bobsled crashed into a tree in Germisch-Partenkirchen, Germany.

Photo Finishes

A drian Moorhouse of Great Britain won the 100-meter breaststroke by one one-hundredth of a second at the 1988 Seoul Olympics. Here are some more exciting photo finishes.

1. GARY HALL, JR., AND ANTHONY ERVIN

Two Americans dead-heated in the 50-meter freestyle swimming competition at the 2000 Sydney Olympics. Gary Hall, Jr., and Anthony Ervin both timed in at 21.98 seconds.

2. NANCY HOGSHEAD AND CARRIE STEINSEIFER

At the 1984 Los Angeles Olympics, Nancy Hogshead and Carrie Steinseifer touched the wall simultaneously at the end of the 100-meter women's freestyle competition. The two Americans were clocked in a time of 55.92 seconds. Each earned a gold medal.

3. JACKSON SCHOLZ

Jackson Scholz of the United States won the gold medal in the 200-meter dash at the 1924 Paris Olympics. Four years later in Amsterdam, Scholz finished tied for third with Germany's Helmuth Körnig in the 200-meters. Rather than give bronze medals to both men, a run-off was proposed by officials. Scholz declined, and Körnig was awarded the bronze medal.

4. EUGENIO MONTI AND LUCIANO DE PAOLIS

The closest two-man bobsled competition in Olympic history occurred at the 1968 Grenoble Winter Olympics. The Italian team of Eugenio Monti and Luciano de Paolis and the Germans Pepi Bader and Horst Floth had a combined four-run time of 4 minutes and 41.54 seconds. The Italians were awarded the gold medal because they had recorded the fastest single run time.

5. JACK KELLER

American Jack Keller and Englishman Donald Finlay finished in a photo for third place in the 110-meter hurdles at the 1932 Los Angeles Olympics. Originally Keller was presented with the bronze medal, but when the judges viewed a film of the race, they realized Finlay had outleaned Keller at the tape. Despite the disappointment, Keller hand-delivered the bronze medal to Donald Finlay.

6. EDDIE TOLAN

The men's 100-meter dash at the 1932 Los Angeles Olympics matched Americans Eddie Tolan and Ralph Metcalfe. The two Americans hit the wire together. Both were timed in 10.3 seconds, an Olympic record. After viewing a film of the race, the judge awarded the gold medal to Tolan, although he and Metcalfe appeared to reach the tape simultaneously.

7. **LINDY REMIGINO**

The finish of the 100-meter dash at the 1952 Helsinki Olympics was the closest in the race's history. Four sprinters were timed at 10.4 seconds. American Lindy Remigino was so convinced that Herb McKenley was the winner that he congratulated the Jamaican. Remigino was shocked when he was informed that he had won the gold medal.

8. **GAIL DEVERS**

American Gail Devers won the gold medal in the women's 100-meter dash at the 1992 Barcelona Olympics. Five sprinters finished within six-hundreths of a second.

9. **THOMAS WASSBERG**

Thomas Wassberg of Sweden won the 15-kilometer alpine skiing competition at the 1980 Lake Placid Winter Olympics. After nearly 42 minutes of skiing, Wassberg edged Juha Mieto of Finland by one one-hundreth of a second.

10. **EDWARD COOKE AND ALFRED GILBERT**

Americans Edward Cooke and Alfred Gilbert both cleared 12 feet, 2 inches in the pole vault at the 1908 London Olympics. Since the marathon was about to finish, it was decided not to have a jump-off to determine the winner. Gilbert and Cooke were awarded gold medals, and three vaulters were presented with bronze medals.

Closing Ceremonies

L et's end the book with a list of notable Olympic lasts.

1. VARASDATES

The last recorded champion of the Ancient Olympics was Varasdates, Prince of Armenia. He won the boxing competition in the year A.D. 369.

2. MARTIN KLEIN

The last Olympic wrestler to win a match that lasted 11 hours was middleweight Martin Klein of Russia. In the early Olympics, Greco-Roman wrestling matches sometimes lasted for hours. The match between Klein and Finland's Alfred Asikainen at the 1912 Stockholm Games seemed as though it would never end. The men took a break every half hour to get a drink of water. After 11 hours, Klein pinned Asikainen. Klein was so tired that he was unable to wrestle in the gold-medal match. Claes Johanson of Sweden won the gold medal by default.

3. **ADOLF SCHMAL**

The last cyclist to win the 12-hour cycling race in the Olympic Games was Austria's Adolf Schmal. The 12-hour race was held for the first and last time at the 1896 Athens Olympics. The race was the last event of the Athens Games. Cyclists had to contend with rain, cold, and gusty winds. The winner was the cyclist who traveled the greatest distance in 12 hours. Schmal covered nearly 180 miles.

4. **ÉMILE THUBRON**

Motor boating was an Olympic competition at the 1908 London Olympics. The winner of the open class was Émile Thubron of France. His boat traveled the 40 nautical miles in 2 hours, 26 minutes, and 53 seconds.

5. **RALPH ROSE**

At the 1912 Stockholm Olympics, there were two-hand competitions in the shot put, javelin, and discus. The athletes would throw with each hand, and the one with the longest combined distance was the winner. The first and last two-hand shot-put winner was American Ralph Rose. His combined throws traveled more than 90 feet.

6. **ROBERT GARRETT**

The last man to win the shot-put competition with a toss of less than 40 feet was Robert Garrett at the 1896 Athens Olympics. The American's winning throw was 36 feet, 9 ¾ inches. The distance was more than 10 feet less than the existing world record. By contrast, the winner of the Olympic shot put today would need a throw of more than 70 feet.

7. **MELVIN SHEPPARD**

The 1,500-meter run is one of the premier events in track and field. The distance is 120 yards short of a mile. The last American man to win the Olympic 1,500 meters was Melvin Sheppard at the 1908 London Games.

8. **1920 FIGURE SKATING COMPETITION**

The first Olympic figure skating competition was held at the 1908 London Summer Games. The last figure skating competition to take place at a Summer Olympics was in 1920 in Antwerp. Four years later, the first Winter Olympics were held in Chamonix.

9. **1908 GREAT BRITAIN TEAM**

Traditionally, Great Britain has not been an Olympic power. The last time England led all nations in gold medals was at the 1908 London Olympics, when the British won 56. Second in the gold-medal count was the United States with 23. When the Olympics returned to London in 1948, the British won only three gold medals.

10. **1936 GERMAN OLYMPICS**

The last time the Summer and Winter Olympics were held in the same country was 1936 in Germany. The Summer Games were staged in Berlin, while the Winter Olympics took place in Garmisch-Partenkirchen. Since the Summer and Winter Olympics no longer occur in the same year, the 1936 German Games may be the last ever held in the same country.

Bibliography

Anderson, Dave. *The Story of the Olympics.* New York: Beech Tree, 1996.

Baker, Eugene. *Olympic Winter Games.* Chicago: Rand McNally & Company, 1979.

Bortstein, Larry. *After Olympic Glory.* New York: Frederick Warne & Company, 1978.

Chester, David. *The Olympic Games Handbook.* New York: Charles Scribner & Sons, 1971.

Collins, Douglas. *Olympic Dreams.* New York: Universe Publishing, 1996.

Connors, Martin, Marie MacNee, Diane Dupuis, and Christa Brelin. *The Olympic Factbook.* Detroit: Visible Ink, 1994.

Daniels, George. *The XIX Olympiad.* Los Angeles: World Sport Research Publications, 1996.

Durant, John. *Highlights of the Olympics.* New York: Hastings House, 1977.

Finley, M. I., and H. W. Pleket. *The Olympic Games: The First Thousand Years.* New York: Viking, 1976.

Galford, Ellen. *The XXIII Olympiad.* Los Angeles: World Sport Research Publications, 1996.

Greenspan, Bud. *100 Greatest Moments in Olympic History.* Urbana: University of Illinois Press, 1992.

Guttmann, Allen. *The Olympics.* Urbana: University of Illinois Press, 1992.

Henry, Bill, and Patricia Henry Yeomans. *An Approved History of the Olympic Games.* Los Angeles: Southern California Committee for the Olympic Games, 1984.

Killanin, Lord, and John Rodda. *The Olympic Games.* New York: Collier, 1976.

Leder, Jane. *Grace and Glory.* Chicago: Triumph Books, 1996.

Mallon, Bill, and Ture Widlund. *The 1896 Olympic Games.* Jefferson, N.C.: McFarland & Company, 1998.

Mallon, Bill. *The 1900 Olympic Games.* Jefferson, N.C.: McFarland & Company, 1998.

Mallon, Bill. *The 1904 Olympic Games.* Jefferson, N.C.: McFarland & Company, 1999.

Mallon, Bill, and Ian Buchannan. *The 1908 Olympic Games.* Jefferson, N.C.: McFarland & Company, 2000.

Phillips, Ellen. *The VIII Olympiad.* Los Angeles: World Sport Research Publications, 1996.

Posey, Carl. *The XVIII Olympiad.* Los Angeles: World Sport Research Publications, 1996.

Siddons, Larry. *The Olympics at 100.* New York: Macmillan, 1995.

Swaddling, Judith. *The Ancient Olympic Games.* Austin: University of Texas Press, 1999.

Wallechinsky, David. *The Complete Book of the Summer Olympics.* Woodstock, N.Y.: Overlook Press, 2000.

Wallechinsky, David. *The Complete Book of the Winter Olympics.* Boston: Little Brown & Company, 1993.

Index

About the Author

Floyd Conner is a lifelong sports fan and the author of many books. His sports books include *Baseball's Most Wanted, More Baseball's Most Wanted, Football's Most Wanted, Basketball's Most Wanted, Golf's Most Wanted, Hockey's Most Wanted, Tennis's Most Wanted, Wrestling's Most Wanted, Day By Day in Cincinnati Bengals History,* and *This Date in Sports History.* He also co-authored *Day By Day in Cincinnati Reds History* and the best-selling *365 Sports Facts a Year Calendar.* He lives in Cincinnati with his wife, Susan, and son, Travis.